MY RESULT BEYOND THE
Finished Line

DEXTER MERCHANT

Copyright © 2024 Dexter Merchant All Rights Reserved

ISBN: 979-8-35098-503-0
eBook ISBN: 979-8-35098-504-7

DEDICATION

I dedicate this the result of this book to my life experiences and the skills I have acquired through reading and researching. Each chapter reflects not only the knowledge I have gained but also the lessons learned from both triumphs and challenges encountered along my journey. The insights shared within these pages culminate years spent exploring diverse fields, engaging with thought leaders, and immersing myself in different literatures that has shaped my understanding of the world.

Additionally, I extend this dedication to my 80 years old mother, Elizabeth Koudy Mamie Merchant, who have provided me with love, motivation, and inspiration throughout my life journey. Her belief in my ability has been a constant source of strength during times of doubt. She always reminded me to continue in pursuit of learning and personal growth and about nurturing relationships that can uplift me. This book stands as a testament to her influence on my journey. My one regret is not being able to give a copy of this finished book to my father, the late John W.S. Merchant,Sr. who life I also exemplify.

Lastly, I dedicate this work to you, the reader who seeks the fulfillment of his/her dreams and the realization of the best results ever. This book is a testament to the power of personal growth and the fulfillment of aspirations. I hope that the ideas presented herein resonate with you and serve as a catalyst for your own growth. May you find encouragement within these pages to pursue your aspirations relentlessly, armed with the knowledge that achieving your best results is not only possible but also within reach.

Towards your best results!

ACKNOWLEDGMENT

Writing a book is often a solitary endeavor, but it is also a journey enriched by many individuals' contributions and support. As I reflect on the creation of *"My Results Beyond the Finished Line"*. I am filled with gratitude for those who have played an integral role in bringing this project to fruition.

To My Family

First and foremost, I would like to express my deepest appreciation to my family. When I look back in the view mirror of life at my children, I do feel a certain fulfillment from the level of Growth and Development in their individual lives. This continues to inspire me to do a little more. Gwendolyn, Dexter jr, Leerod, Bobby, Dexterlyn, Renedell and Jasmine and not forgetting their mother, Twegbarlee Serena Merchant, the original this what I called the driving force. Thank you all for the inspiration.

To My Team members and Colleagues

I am immensely grateful to my mentors and colleagues who have guided me through this journey. Your insights and constructive feedback have shaped not only this book but also my perspective as a writer. A special thanks to Genevie Fahnbulleh my partner at the Secure Future Enterprise and the Executive Director for the Secure Women Organization for her patience during the countless hours I spent writing and revising. Her trust and belief in me to get this task complete has been a constant source of motivation.

To My Readers

To all potential readers, thank you for your interest in *"My Results Beyond the Finished Line." I* hope that this book resonates with you, inspires you, and encourages you to reflect on your own journeys beyond conventional endpoints. Your engagement with this work is what ultimately gives it purpose.

To My Editors and Publishing Team

A heartfelt thank you goes out to my editors. Your meticulous attention to detail has transformed rough drafts into polished prose. The collaborative spirit we shared during the editing process was instrumental in enhancing the clarity and impact of this book.

FORWARD

In an age where instant gratification often overshadows the value of hard work and dedication, "My Result Beyond the Finished Line" emerges as a vital guide for those seeking to redefine their understanding of success. This self-help motivational book is not just about reaching goals; it's about embracing the journey that leads us there and recognizing that true fulfillment lies in continuous growth and learning.

This book provides readers with practical tools and insights to establish clear, meaningful objectives that resonate with their core values. By encouraging individuals to set ambitious yet attainable goals, it lays the groundwork for a purposeful journey, reminding us that every step taken is significant.

As we traverse our paths, challenges are inevitable. "My Result Beyond the Finished Line" emphasizes the importance of perseverance—the unwavering commitment to push through obstacles. Through compelling stories and relatable examples, readers will learn how resilience can be nurtured, transforming setbacks into steppingstones toward greater achievements.

It invites readers to transform the way they perceive success, turning every milestone into a powerful launchpad for a life of purpose, growth, and resilience. This book breaks through the traditional notion of the "finish line" and inspires readers to explore what lies on the other side of achievement—those deeper, life-altering results that fuel long-term fulfillment.

With a blend of heartfelt storytelling and actionable guidance, it empowers readers to view each success as a steppingstone toward even greater accomplishments, both personal and professional. Readers will discover how to build an unshakable mindset, nurture resilience, and see challenges as catalysts for growth, allowing them to turn limitations into boundless opportunities.

In conclusion, this book serves as both an inspirational companion and a practical guide for anyone eager to find deeper meaning in their pursuits. It reminds us that while crossing the finish line may signify achievement, it also marks the beginning of new adventures—each filled with opportunities for further exploration and self-discovery. Happy Reading and Guidance!

ABOUT THE AUTHOR

Mr. Dexter Merchant is an Agile Results-Based Knowledge Management Specialist, Coach, and Consultant with extensive experience in public engagement and social entrepreneur development. With a career spanning over two decades, Mr. Merchant has honed his expertise as a Performance Technocrat, dedicating  the last five years to research development, Building Human Resource Capacity and stronger communities. His multifaceted approach combines theoretical knowledge with practical application, allowing him to address complex challenges in various sectors effectively.

Throughout his career, Mr. Merchant has been involved in numerous donor-funded projects that have significantly impacted communities and individuals facing adversity. Notably, he contributed to the World Bank project to empower vulnerable women in fragile states, which is a testament to his commitment to social equity and sustainable development. His work extends to youth development initiatives, where he has implemented innovative strategies that foster resilience and growth among young people.

In addition to his project management skills, Mr. Merchant is recognized for his ability to monitor and evaluate programs effectively. This skill set enables him to assess the impact of interventions critically and ensure that resources are allocated efficiently for maximum benefit. His insights into learning strategies have also made him a sought-after coach for organizations looking to enhance their performance through knowledge management practices, through his community, Real-TimeResultsAcademy.org and the securefuturecommunity.org.

Mr. Merchant, who is also a motivational speaker, and from his deep understanding of the root causes of poverty and social inequality believes that systemic change is necessary for individuals to escape the cycle of poverty and achieve their fullest potential. Through this book, he shares a wealth of experiences drawn from personal anecdotes and rigorous research on achieving tangible results in various contexts.

His writing not only reflects his professional journey but also serves as an inspiration for those seeking guidance in navigating the complexities of social entrepreneurship and community engagement. By combining empirical evidence with heartfelt narratives, Mr. Merchant aims to empower readers with actionable insights that can lead to meaningful change.

In summary, Mr. Dexter Merchant stands out as a dedicated advocate for social change whose extensive background in knowledge management, coaching, and evaluation equips him uniquely to address pressing societal issues while inspiring others on their journeys beyond their finished line.

TABLE OF CONTENTS

Getting Started Why we Start and Don't Finish—and How to Break Through 1
    The Drop-off Effect: Why We Don't Reach the Finish Line 2
    The Cost of Unfinished Goals 2
    Going Beyond the Finish Line 3

Chapter 1 Introduction 5
    Human Reproduction and Life Stages 6
    Navigating Life's Phases with Purpose 6
    The Imperative Need for Continuous Improvement 7
    Encouragement for Taking Action Towards Desired Results 8
    Letter to Readers 8
    Transformation into a Result-Oriented Individual 8
    Realizing Desired Results 9
    Journey of Self-Discovery 9
    Embracing Smart Work for Goal Attainment 9
    Sharing Success with Others 9
    Getting started 12
    Can you learn any lessons from my story? 13

Chapter 2 Because you have already paid the life premium 19
    You Paid Life Its Dividend Over Time 19
    Have You Already Paid Life's Premium Price? 20
    Reaping Life's Equity 20
    Demand Your Fair Share 20
    Lessons Learned on the Universe's Stage 21
    The Value of Experience Over Perfection 21
    Resilience in Adversity 22
    Embracing Action and Learning 22
    The Impact of Life's Experiences on Our Development 23
    The Toll Life Takes on Us 23

Demanding Worth from Our Suffering 23

Wisdom Through Struggles 24

Shaping Our Paths 24

Viewing Obstacles as Opportunities 24

Always Solve Problems That You Care About 25

Perceive the Problem and Reduce Its Impact 25

Trigger Your Passion 25

Build on Your Strengths 26

Address Potentially Large Concerns Timely 26

Build on What Could Get Better 26

Avoid Reinventing the Wheel 26

Learning from Others 27

The Success Language 27

Did You Get the True Sense of it? 29

Procrastination 30

Imagine Walking a Dark Path 31

The Power of Illumination 32

Choosing to Use Your Light 32

Navigating Challenges Effectively 32

Money Relationship as a Means to an End 33

Awareness of Thoughts and Opinions about Money 35

Communication with Money 35

The Consequences of Ruthlessness 35

Building Trust with Your Finances 36

Chapter 3 A Purpose in Life 37

The Joy of Giving: A Deeper Exploration 37

The Essence of Giving 37

The Psychological Benefits 38

Finding Purpose Through Generosity 38

The Importance of Having a Sense of Purpose 38

Motivation and Engagement 39

Prioritization and Accomplishment 39

Connection and Community 39
Consequences of Lacking Purpose 40
Pursue Your Purpose No Matter the Delayed Outcome 40
Overcoming Negative Self-Talk: A Path to Empowerment 41
So, Break Yourself Free! 41
Understanding the Need for Professional Help in
Overcoming Negative Thoughts and Beliefs 42
Do You Have All the Facts? 43
Do You Really Believe Every Word? The Information Overload of Today ... 45
The Importance of Reliable Information in Decision-Making 46
Take the Small Steps 47
Do Not Rely on Yourself 48
The Importance of Open-Mindedness in Evaluating Situations 49
Widen Your Perspective 50
Can Anything Good Come Out of Nazarene? 52

Chapter 4 Five Important life management questions to answer 53

1. What? 53
2. Why 55
3. Who? 58
4. The How? 60
5. The When? 63

Chapter 5 Changing Circumstances 66

Regaining Control 66
Creating a New Routine 67
Finding Balance 67
Building Support Networks 67
Have you become discouraged? 68
The Struggle with Overwhelming Demands of Life 69
Do Strong Feelings Consume You? 71
What Can You Do About It? 71
The Importance of Connection 72
Recommended Tips for Managing Negative Feelings 72

Bottom Line: Perspective Matters 73
You Can Change Your Current Circumstances 73

Chapter 6 The Energy of Determination 75
The Role of Belief Systems in Achievement 78
Finished what you start 80
Keeping Pace With Time 81
The Importance of Standing for Something 83
A Call to Action 84

Chapter 7 The Power of Perseverance 85
Cultivating a Positive Mindset Toward Your Best Results 87
What is a Growth Mindset? 88
Negative Self-Talk and Its Effects 88
Did You Complete What You Started? 90
The Importance of Standing for Something 92
A call to action 93

Chapter 8 Understanding Prioritization 94
The Importance of Decision-Making 95
Choosing Your Focus 95
Clarity and Priorities 95
Be Firm in Decision Making 96
Taking Responsibility and Accountability 97
Understanding Your SWOT Analysis 98
The Importance of Continuous Learning 99
Take Action 100
Disconnect from Negative Influence 100
Understanding a Farmer's Work and his own success 101
Creating a Positive Environment for Growth 101
The Importance of Choosing Our Influences 101
Impact of Dissenting Opinions 102
The Result Problem Tree 103
Identifying the Root Cause 104

Identifying the Main Problem 104
Recognizing the Effects 104
Taking Action: How to Overcome Challenges 105
A Life Project Approach 106
The Importance of Monitoring Progress 106
Investing Time Wisely 106
Tracking Progress Towards Goals 106
Setting Key Performance Indicators (KPIs) 107
Making Changes Based on Feedback 107
Treating Life as a Project 107
Planning and Evaluation in Personal Growth 108

Chapter 9 Overcoming Challenges 109

Facing Fear and Doubt 109
Understanding Fear and Doubt 109
Face Fear and Doubt Heads On 110
Real-Life Examples of Overcoming Challenges 110
Learning From Failures 111
Strategies to Learn from Failure 111
Real-Life Examples of Resilience 112
Bouncing Back is Stronger 112
Strategies to Build Resilience 112
Real-Life Examples 113
Facing Challenges for Success 113
The Importance of Clear Motives 114
The Role of Dissatisfaction in Change 114
Building a Strong Mindset 115
The Importance of Effort 115

Chapter 10 Results Beyond the Finished Line- Embracing new path? 117

The Conclusion
Embrace Your Journey Beyond the Finish Line 120
- Embrace the Power of Proactivity 121
- Breaking Habits and Embracing Change 122
- Embrace a Positive Mindset 122
- Take Action and Engage 123
- Learn from Experience 123
- Prioritize and Invest in your self 123
- Cultivate Ambition 124
- Investing in ourselves: A Path to Health and Wealth 124
- Embrace Life and Purpose to the end 125

GETTING STARTED

WHY WE START AND DON'T FINISH— AND HOW TO BREAK THROUGH

So many people begin their journey toward a goal full of motivation and drive, yet somehow, they never quite make it to the end. Research shows this isn't just a personal challenge; it's a global one. Whether it's starting a new business, setting New Year's resolutions, signing up for an online course, or joining a gym, the pattern is often the same: we set out with purpose, but somewhere along the way, our resolve fades, and our goal becomes another abandoned project.

In My Result Beyond the Finish Line, we will explore why so many people fall short of their goals and, more importantly, how to go the distance. With the right mindset and strategies, it's possible to push beyond the obstacles that trip up so many and achieve results that go beyond what we thought possible. Below are some startling statistics that illustrate the global struggle to turn intentions into actions and how common it is to lose momentum.

The Drop-off Effect: Why We Don't Reach the Finish Line

Studies reveal that only about 8-10% of people keep their New Year's resolutions for an entire year, meaning that by February, a staggering 80% have already let their goals slip. This pattern is universal, extending beyond New Year's intentions to almost every kind of goal or project we might start. From creative pursuits to entrepreneurial dreams, the drop-off effect has a way of turning excitement into regret.

For instance, in the world of entrepreneurship, 50% of new businesses in the United States close within five years. Worldwide, over 90% of startups are never completed or reach true sustainability. Many of these ventures fail not because the ideas are unworthy but because initial enthusiasm fades when reality hits. As human beings, we tend to lose steam when the results are slow to materialize or when the hurdles feel too high to overcome.

And it's not just in business—our personal goals suffer as well. In fitness, for instance, 63% of gym memberships go unused, and 50% of new gym-goers quit within six months. So, what is the common thread in all these statistics? A universal difficulty in maintaining consistency, finding focus, and pushing through the setbacks.

The Cost of Unfinished Goals

The cost of abandoning goals isn't just about missed opportunities. Each time we start something but fail to complete it, it reinforces a pattern of stopping short. Every abandoned project can leave a lingering feeling of disappointment or even a belief that "I just can't finish what I start." This is a mindset that can be shifted but requires a new approach—one that emphasizes resilience and pushing "beyond the finish line."

One area that highlights this struggle is online learning. Completion rates for online courses are as low as 5-15%, globally and in the United States. People begin with great intentions, hoping to upskill or pursue new knowledge, but quickly find themselves overwhelmed or distracted. Does any of these statistics resonate with you? Today, that will change for good. The low completion rate is a stark reminder that while starting is important, finishing is essential to real growth and results.

Going Beyond the Finish Line

So how can we be the few who push through and achieve? In My Result Beyond the Finish Line, we'll focus on actionable strategies that can help you become one of the 8-10% who reach their resolutions, the 10% of startups that make it, and the committed few who don't give up on self-improvement or personal growth. It's not about forcing ourselves to reach the finish line; it's about redefining what it means to finish. It's about looking beyond the endpoint and making each effort, no matter how small, a steppingstone to our ultimate vision beyond the finish line.

As you read this book, keep in mind these statistics as reminders of the common pitfalls. But know that each chapter will arm you with the tools to push through these barriers, to find your unique results beyond the finish line, and to live with purpose, resilience, and a commitment that takes you farther than you ever imagined.

CHAPTER 1
INTRODUCTION

"To the writing of many books, there is no end, and much devotion to them is worrisome to the soul." – **King Solomon**

To the writing of many books....

Books have served as a primary medium for preserving and transmitting knowledge across generations. They have allowed societies to build upon the achievements of their predecessors and avoid repeating past mistakes.

In this context, books are more than just physical objects; they are repositories of wisdom and cultural

heritage. By reading and engaging with these texts, individuals can gain insights into the thoughts, values, and beliefs of people from different times and places.

Yes, to the writing of many books, there is no end, and this writing "Result beyond the finish line, in the game of life" will surely last a lifetime. The lesson learned from Result Beyond the finish line will be applied from generation to generation.

It is most often believed that teachers, especially those with more experience in practical life lessons, can leave a lasting impression and impact. Therefore, you can experience firsthand the huge lessons learned from living in real-life situations and apply them for your own good. These lessons have already been processed, so they are good for consumption.

Every individual is believed to have a unique purpose or mission to fulfill during their time on Earth. This purpose is often seen as the driving force behind one's actions, decisions, and contributions to society. Just like a project, life can be viewed as having a cyclical nature, with a clear beginning and end. This cyclical nature is evident in the natural progression of human life from conception to death.

Human Reproduction and Life Stages

Throughout this book, I have mentioned the natural cycle of human reproduction as a metaphor for the broader journey of life. It starts with the fertilization of an egg cell, leading to conception. This moment marks the beginning of a new life, which then goes through various stages, such as gestation in the womb for approximately nine months before birth occurs. After birth, individuals go through the stages of infancy, childhood, adolescence, adulthood, and old age and eventually face mortality.

Navigating Life's Phases with Purpose

Each life phase presents its own challenges, opportunities, and experiences that shape an individual's journey. Navigating these phases purposefully involves setting goals, making choices aligned with one's values and aspirations, overcoming obstacles, learning from failures and successes, and making meaningful contributions to others and society. By approaching each stage with intentionality and mindfulness, individuals can strive to create a legacy that reflects their values, beliefs, achievements, and impact on others.

Life is a continuous journey that challenges us to strive for excellence as we align ourselves with our true purpose. It is essential to harness our energies efficiently at every juncture of our existence. Whether we are brimming with the vitality of youth or enriched with the sagacity of old age, each phase Presents distinct opportunities for us to realize our purpose and leave a lasting impact on the world. This approach to life underscores the significance of personal growth, perpetual learning, and the unwavering pursuit of our aspirations. By adopting this mindset, we ensure that our narrative is characterized by accomplishments and a profound sense of purpose.

The Imperative Need for Continuous Improvement

In today's fast-paced world, there is an escalating necessity to enhance both the methods we employ and the reasons driving our actions. The currency of the present moment lies in the tangible outcomes we achieve in our individual lives. Striving for superior results has the power to positively transform our current circumstances and propels us towards a future brimming with possibilities. It is imperative to extend kindness towards oneself, eschew excuses, overcome self-imposed barriers, and take decisive steps toward realizing desired outcomes. By prioritizing immediate results and taking proactive measures, individuals pave the way for personal growth and success.

Encouragement for Taking Action Towards Desired Results

I commend you for investing your time in absorbing this motivational discourse—a testament to your commitment to attaining your desired outcomes. This act signifies a bold stride toward seizing control of your destiny and steering it toward favorable results. Remember that progress is rooted in action; therefore, I urge you to shed self-doubt, eliminate procrastination, and embrace a proactive stance in pursuing your goals. By embracing this ethos of action - oriented determination, you set yourself on a trajectory marked by achievements and fulfillment.

Letter to Readers

I am excited to present to you an incredible opportunity in the form of a motivational reading material called "Result beyond the Finish Line." This book is designed to transform your mindset and make you more result-oriented. Upon immersing yourself in its contents, you will undergo a profound change and start viewing your life through the lens of achieving tangible outcomes.

> **Letter to readers**
>
> *After reading and digesting this book, you will not be the same person—you will become a result-oriented person (disclaimer).*
>
> *Because you deserved to be happy you will not allow a fight with someone to affect your mood and performance for the rest of the day, weeks, months or perhaps the rest of your life.*

Transformation into a Result-Oriented Individual

Upon absorbing the wisdom contained within "Result beyond the Finish Line," you will witness a significant shift in your approach towards life. The principles outlined in this book are geared towards helping you unlock your full potential and guiding you towards attaining the results you aspire to achieve.

Realizing Desired Results

By implementing the strategies elucidated in this book, you will envision and actualize the outcomes you desire for your life. It will empower you to treat your life as a project demanding nurturing and growth, enabling you to thrive in all aspects.

Journey of Self-Discovery

"Result beyond the Finish Line" is a companion on your journey of self-discovery and realization of your life's true worth. It acts as a roadmap that leads you towards uncovering and harnessing your hidden capabilities to manifest the results that align with your aspirations.

Embracing Smart Work for Goal Attainment

Are you ready to embrace a smarter approach towards setting and achieving your life's results? If so, embark on this transformative journey by boarding the Result train. There is ample space for everyone on this voyage towards personal growth and success.

Sharing Success with Others

As you begin witnessing positive changes in your own life, extend a helping hand to your friends and family by sharing your experiences with them. Encourage them to embark on their own journeys towards realizing their desired results, fostering a community of individuals committed to personal development.

Get on board the result train

We are all dynamic and passionate beings. When one area of our lives suffers, other areas can still be explored and nurtured. Thinking through your options and alternatives is essential to making things happen for you. You deserve to be happy, so don't let a conflict with someone affect your mood and performance for the rest of the day, weeks, months, or perhaps even the rest of your life. Resolve the issue, make amends, and move forward, or place those problems in a metaphorical parking lot.

In life, resilience is key. Even when faced with setbacks or challenges in one aspect of our lives, we have the capacity to shift our focus and energy to other areas where we can still thrive and find fulfillment. Maintaining a balanced perspective and prioritizing our well-being ensures that temporary obstacles do not derail our happiness and progress. Address conflicts with empathy and understanding, but also recognize when it's time to set them aside and continue on your path. Life is too short to be weighed down by unresolved issues; embrace the dynamic nature of your existence and keep moving forward with passion and purpose.

If we genuinely want to live our best life, the key is to have all significant areas of life working harmoniously together. This is precisely what I will show you in this book. The fact that you are reading this book means you have already taken the opportune time for yourself because you don't have time to waste on non-essential activities that do not add value.

Until you address the root cause of your problems, you'll never be able to break the cycle of not having enough time and feeling constantly overwhelmed and stressed. If you are still hesitant that this book, "Result beyond the finished line" is a good reading", continue reading and I can assure you that by reading and applying its content, you will begin to see that:

- You can achieve greater success in your life.
- You can attain better life balance.
- You can improve relationships with those you care about.
- You can become wealthier and have more enthusiasm and energy.
- Overall, you can live the life you truly desire.

Your success is a **"do it yourself project."** But if you look further, you might find people and resources that are more than available to help you along the way, like this book: **Result Beyond the Finish Line**

Happy Reading!

Getting started

Dexter Merchant, Author

Lessons from my case study show the process, experience acquired over 25 years, and actual life experience. The penning down of this book spanned over 10 years ago, right after the Ebola crisis in Liberia around May 2014. The project to write this book could have been aborted prematurely if I was not motivated and passionate about writing my story and encouraging people to view life positively. To fulfill that purpose, I needed to set realistic goals and take major steps to achieve them.

Now that you have found yourself in the right focus to read this piece of literature, you can look forward to a very rewarding future since my story is built on the same side of the coin. My students, mentors, and children have read through this book. They are now following through to fulfill their true purpose in life. The fact that you have reached this far shows that you can finish this book and find your true-life purpose.

One secret I would like to share with you is that once you get started, you will soon begin to think more successfully about attracting wealth and developing a good relationship with money even before you finish reading this book, My Result Beyond the Finished Line. Get started and take the needed action for your best results

THE ROOT CAUSE

…….Because until you address the root cause of your problem, you'll never be able to break the cycle of not having enough time and feeling constantly overwhelmed, stressed out and not living the life you really wanted to.

ever. All these rich experiences and insights that are published in this book will be meaningless if it is not read and followed through. Your job now is to read it thoroughly from cover to cover to apply the sense of it.

Can you learn any lessons from my story?

My story is not just a story, but a guide to help you reach your desired destination. It could be an eye-opener. To reach this far in pursuing my true purpose, I read over 20 pieces of motivational books, visited many websites and blogs, and attended workshops, seminars, and webinars. I did all this to identify my true purpose, so you don't have to reinvent the wheel. I've condensed all these experiences and materials in this book making it a credible source for your personal growth.

One painful moment of my life was the day my daughter called me from her school campus one morning saying that she was asked to leave the class session because she was due school fees for that semester. The pain that got me during that particular moment of my life was too much to bear, and quickly, I said to myself, is this not the same school my daughter attended during the last 10 years? During these past years, there has been no time when this kind of embarrassment has come to me because I paid her fees on time. The circumstances were different this time since I was broke. I reason that money was the tool or antidote I needed at that moment to keep her in school, and if I wanted to maintain that relationship with the school and keep my daughter in class, it meant that I must pay up their money (debt), period.

That turning point was the beginning of my new outlook on money and success. I learned the hard way that having money is part of our lives and is truly a means to an end, and it is surely a form of protection. So, being

> *…….I learned the hard way that family and business spending do not blend well. It is like mixing Fuel and water.*

more aware of your thoughts and opinions about money is like keeping a good relationship.

Let me ask you this question again: *Do you really speak thoughtlessly or worthlessly about your good relationship?*

To be honest, I am not sure. Therefore, I recommend being nice to your money relationship, enticing it, and attracting it more and more.

Now, let's consider another perspective. What do you do when your electronic device can't work well because of a virus? Your first option is not getting rid of your piece of equipment, but you will rather perceive that the virus is a threat to your equipment, and you need to get that antivirus scan, clean it up, and keep it going. And this is exactly what you will do. In the same manner, the lack of money is a threat, and like a virus, it is a threat to our life sustenance, so you need that antivirus to clean it up and keep moving. Could this book become an anti-virus?

I reckon that to have a friendship with money and let it work for me, I needed to borrow it/take a loan to get into business. This is exactly what I did, but this led to bigger debt due to a lack of business sense and heavier external family debts and responsibility, and at the same time, trying to play a nicer guy. I learned the hard way that family and business spending do not blend well. It is like mixing Fuel and water. Later, I did more research and came across many writings, such as a book called MNL Aloe Vera Marketing, the Law of Attraction, connective Learning, and the like.

Something in me said I could do better putting the best wine in a broken glass bottle, but it would be wasteful.

> ………..*My passion for training led to the quest that put me in 5 different class rooms- teaching grade school students, secondary, college and university students and running these curriculums and syllabus simultaneously.*

By this time, I was already 45 years old. So, I started to do more reading and get motivated. It was when I came to realize that the road to true wealth is to get the results you truly desire. Although there could be a lot of variables, thinking straight on the path of true success and acting on it is a way forward to attaining your true purpose. I also noticed that success could happen more quickly in our lives if no procrastination syndrome prevented us from moving forward. I called that the old man procrastination syndrome, which also hampered my own movement on many fronts. Even when I began putting my thoughts and my experiences on paper in the book "Result Beyond the Finished Line," the procrastination syndrome was my worst nightmare.

Don't let that happen to you... Make that move now!

The Law of Attraction says that "everyone can do it, and everyone should try".

In order to attain my best results and fulfill my life purpose, I scuffle to fill some needs over the years by assisting hundreds of people find their own purpose and get some of their best results ever. I did this through training, facilitating workshops, putting young people on the job training, getting them on surveys, and working as enumerators. My passion for training led to the quest that put me in 5 different classrooms – teaching grade school students, secondary, college, and university students and running these curriculums and syllabi simultaneously.

My quest to find my true purpose also led me to develop a sense of success through becoming an entrepreneur. This business sense led me to establish in my mind and head and then on the ground first "The Merchant Investment Company, The Deo-volente Collections, DV Balloons, Guess House management service, The Center for Productivity Manpower Development (CEPMDE), The Secure Future Enterprise, and My Result Now Consulting among others. This time period spans over 25 years of doing many different things to have a good relationship with money. There were inconsistencies, loss of focus, and directions as I was punching the air and missing the mark for my true purpose.

> ......*Actually, if we continue in the same routine, we will get the same results- only athletes do this and get better results*

I realized that I needed more of the entrepreneur's blood and impetus to change things around if I truly wanted to succeed. Moreinformation, knowledge, training, real – life experience, focus, objectives, and goals had to be acquired and set to get the wire up. So, to get the needed training and direction, I took up more jobs consulting and leading projects for others, making them successful. This way, I was able to learn endurance. I also discovered that to be truly successful is not just having a mindset but leading it into your way of living – the daily actions and activities you engage in. I have met so many people in my different work life. Over the years, I have been known as The Manager, Director, M&E Specialist, Wisdom, Results, Papay pressure, Uncle D", Bossman, OIC, Specialist, M&E specialist, Evaluator, Data manager, project developer, and social entrepreneur.

I also discovered that our brains are conditioned to succeed and enjoy life, so you must use them to attain success. Actually, if we continue in the same routine, we will get the same results. Only athletes do this and get better results. I have done research on YouTube, watched videos, followed successful people, written scripts, and reconditioned my thoughts to enter what I want to call the "success mode."

Success mode is about intentionally rewiring your mindset to focus on growth and achievement. It's not just about hard work; it's about smart work, learning from those who've already paved the way. It's about creating a mental environment where success is the only option, and failure is merely a stepping stone to greater accomplishments. Embracing this mindset has transformed my approach to challenges and opportunities, making every step a deliberate move toward a more fulfilling and successful life.

WRITTEN THOUGHTS

> *............I found out that when pieces of thoughts are written down instead of kept in memory, you retain the actual origin and when put together it expresses a complete thought.*

I jump up each night to write down thoughts coming through my subconscious mind. I continue to do this as new thoughts unfold. I found out that when pieces of thoughts are written down instead of kept in memory, you retain the actual origin and express a complete thought when put together. I also discovered that we are here to fill a need and to help us achieve this, we must learn how to attract and get our own potion of wealth and abundance that this world has to offer.

The information contained here can energize you to jumpstart your journey toward true financial freedom and the best results ever. Keep reading. If you keep reading, I promise you will never be the same again. Don't stop now, and don't let the old man's procrastination slow you down or stop you. Keep moving forward. Don't stand in front of your best results by blocking your own path. Don't be the cause of your own stumbling. Have you not heard that no one who puts their hand to a project and then turns back finishes it?

The rains are coming; the storm is on its way, and so is the snow. Even if darkness overshadows you, now is the time to move ahead. Trust me, you will not regret it. I know exactly the negative effects of procrastination. It slows you down and makes you put off things that could be completed in record time. This was one of the reasons it took me nearly five years to complete this book.

If this book, "My Result Beyond the Finished Line," had been completed four years ago, thousands of purposeful people like you would have been living the life of the dream with the financial security you really deserved. So, you do not have to take four years to finish reading this book before taking action to change your life and fulfill the purpose and needs you were born to fulfill. This is a map of my life; *have you discovered yours?*

- Creativity
- Motivation
- Planning ability
- Inspirational
- Always seeking ways to help

This story will be told for a long time to come. Can you write yours?

CHAPTER 2
BECAUSE YOU HAVE ALREADY PAID THE LIFE PREMIUM

It is written: "Which of you, wanting to build a house, will not first calculate the cost?" I discovered that we all do things differently to succeed. But maybe if we work smarter, we could be better off with our life purpose by calculating the cost.

Let me share your sorrow, your pain, and your grief. Let me help carry the burden with you as you read on. The cost can be so great. We need each other here, so continue reading.

Look, I've got some thought-provoking questions for you. Have you paid life its dividend over time? Have you already paid Life's premium price? If so, then the time that has passed is sufficient for you to have remained in a state of lacking the things you need to make you and your family happy. Because it is time to begin reaping its equity as inequitable distribution. Demand your fair share… reap life's dividends while still breathing.

You Paid Life Its Dividend Over Time

Life, in its essence, is a complex tapestry woven from experiences, choices, and the passage of time. When we ask ourselves whether we have paid life its dividend over time, we are essentially reflecting on the investments we have made emotionally, physically, and spiritually in our journey through existence. These dividends can manifest in various forms: personal happiness, relationship fulfillment, professional achievements, and overall well-being. Each moment spent nurturing these aspects contributes to a cumulative effect that can either enrich our lives or leave us feeling impoverished.

Have You Already Paid Life's Premium Price?

The concept of paying life's premium price suggests that every choice comes with costs. Sacrifices made for career advancement may lead to missed family moments; pursuing passions might require financial investment or time away from other responsibilities. The question invites introspection about whether the sacrifices we've made align with our true desires and values. Have you invested enough in your happiness? Have you prioritized your needs alongside those of your family? If you find yourself reflecting on these questions with a sense of regret or unfulfillment, it may indicate that the premium has been paid but not fully appreciated.

Reaping Life's Equity

If indeed you have paid this premium over time and yet feel deprived of essential joys and satisfactions, it is crucial to recognize that the time elapsed should not be viewed merely as a period of waiting but rather as an opportunity for growth and realization. The notion of reaping equity speaks to the idea that life offers returns based on what one has sown. If you feel that your contributions have not yielded adequate rewards be it love, joy, security, or peace it is imperative to take action. This inequitable distribution of life's blessings often stems from societal norms or personal barriers that prevent individuals from claiming their rightful share.

Demand Your Fair Share

To demand your fair share means advocating for yourself and acknowledging your worthiness of happiness and fulfillment. It involves recognizing that life is not merely about enduring hardships but also about celebrating victories big and small. It encourages a proactive approach: setting boundaries where necessary, pursuing passions unapologetically, and fostering connections that uplift rather than drain you. By doing so while still breathing while still engaged in the vibrant act of living you position yourself to experience life more fully.

In conclusion, if you resonate with the sentiment that you've been lacking what truly makes you happy despite having invested significant time and effort into life's journey, now is the moment to reclaim what is rightfully yours. Embrace the idea that it is never too late to start reaping life's dividends; take charge of your narrative and ensure that each day moving forward reflects your aspirations for joy and fulfillment.

Lessons Learned on the Universe's Stage

Through all these years, what lessons have you been able to pick up during your groaning process on the universe's stage? This question invites a deep reflection on personal growth and the wisdom gained through experiences, particularly in the pursuit of financial freedom. The journey toward achieving true financial independence is often fraught with challenges, setbacks, and learning opportunities.

The Value of Experience Over Perfection

In this context, it is crucial to recognize that *getting your fingers burnt while pursuing true financial freedom is better than letting your whole body burn in the process.* This metaphor emphasizes the importance of taking calculated risks and learning from mistakes rather than avoiding action altogether due to fear of failure. Each setback can serve as a valuable lesson that contributes to personal development and resilience. The scars we bear from our experiences can be seen as badges of honor that signify our willingness to engage with life fully, despite its inherent uncertainties.

Resilience in Adversity

The phrase "a wounded lion is better than a dead elephant" encapsulates the essence of resilience. It suggests that even in a state of injury or struggle, there is still strength and potential for recovery. A wounded lion can still fight back and reclaim its position, whereas a dead elephant represents a finality that leaves no room for growth or redemption. This perspective encourages individuals to embrace their struggles as part of their journey rather than viewing them as insurmountable obstacles.

Embracing Action and Learning

Ultimately, you now go experience and get it done. This call to action underscores the necessity of stepping out of one's comfort zone and actively engaging with life's challenges. It highlights that knowledge alone is insufficient; practical application through experience is where real learning occurs. By taking initiative and facing fears head-on, individuals can cultivate skills, build confidence, and develop a deeper understanding of themselves and their aspirations.

In summary, the lessons learned through years of navigating life's complexities revolve around embracing risk, cultivating resilience in adversity, and prioritizing action over inaction. Each experience whether it results in success or failure contributes to a richer understanding of oneself and paves the way toward achieving true financial freedom.

This book when fully read as a motivational tool can revive your wounded state, rejuvenate your mission, and prepare you to challenge yourself toward fulfilling your true purpose and realizing the need you were born to fulfill.

The Impact of Life's Experiences on Our Development

The experiences we acquire over time are shown by the number of strokes and blows life has given us. Each encounter, whether joyous or painful, contributes to the tapestry of our existence, weaving together a narrative that is uniquely ours. These experiences manifest in various ways; sometimes they are evident in our facial expressions and lines etched into our skin that tell stories of laughter and sorrow alike. Other times, they reveal themselves through our thoughts, which may oscillate between hope and despair, reflecting the duality of human experience. Our fears often serve as reminders of past traumas or failures, while our physiology can bear the marks of stress and resilience sleepless nights leading to dark circles under our eyes, baldness as a testament to worry, gray hair signaling wisdom gained through hardship, and wrinkles that narrate tales of joy and grief.

The Toll Life Takes on Us

Life will take its toll on us many sleepless nights filled with anxiety about the future or regrets about the past can accumulate like layers upon layers of sediment in a riverbed. The physical manifestations of this toll are not merely superficial; they represent deeper emotional and psychological battles fought over time. Each wrinkle can symbolize a lesson learned or a moment cherished; each gray hair may signify wisdom earned through trials faced head-on. Pain becomes an inevitable companion on this journey, reminding us that growth often comes at a cost.

Demanding Worth from Our Suffering

But I often realize that when we pay these prices, we can demand the worth of our suffering and pain from life. This realization is pivotal it transforms passive endurance into active engagement with our circumstances. We let life know that from our SMART (Specific, Measurable, Achievable, Relevant, Time-bound) actions, we deserve more than mere survival; we seek fulfillment and purpose. By setting clear goals for ourselves based on the lessons learned from past struggles, we assert our agency in shaping our destinies rather than being mere victims of circumstance.

Wisdom Through Struggles

These ups and downs pains and struggles make us wise. They help us finish our training in the school of life where every challenge serves as an instructor imparting valuable lessons. Wisdom is not simply knowledge accumulated over time but rather an understanding forged through experience the ability to navigate complexities with grace and insight. As we learn from each setback or triumph, we become better equipped to guide others who follow in our footsteps.

Shaping Our Paths

They shape both ourselves and those who follow our lead, making our paths straight. The journey is not solitary; it influences those around us friends, family members, and colleagues who observe how we respond to adversity. Our resilience can inspire them to face their challenges with courage and determination. In this way, we become beacons of hope for others navigating their tumultuous waters.

Viewing Obstacles as Opportunities

The blows, punches, and impediments life places before us should not be viewed as stumbling blocks but rather as stepping stones to higher heights. Each obstacle presents an opportunity for growth a chance to reassess priorities or develop new skills that propel us forward rather than hold us back. Embracing this perspective allows us to cultivate a mindset rooted in possibility rather than limitation.

In conclusion, while life's experiences may leave visible marks on us both physically and emotionally, they also provide invaluable lessons that contribute significantly to personal development. By recognizing the worth inherent in our suffering and using it as fuel for growth, we can transform challenges into opportunities for greater wisdom and strength.

Always Solve Problems That You Care About

When embarking on the journey of problem-solving, it is crucial to focus on issues that resonate with you. This intrinsic motivation not only fuels your commitment but also enhances your creativity and resourcefulness in finding solutions. When you care about a problem, you are more likely to invest the necessary time and energy into understanding its nuances and complexities. This emotional connection can lead to innovative approaches that might not surface if you were merely addressing a problem out of obligation or external pressure.

Perceive the Problem and Reduce Its Impact

To effectively tackle any issue, one must first perceive it. This involves analyzing the problem from multiple angles to understand its root causes and implications fully. Once you have a comprehensive view, the next step is to strategize on how to mitigate its impact. This could involve developing practical solutions that address immediate concerns while also considering long-term effects. By reducing the impact of a problem, you create space for growth and improvement, both for yourself and those affected by the issue.

Trigger Your Passion

The problems you choose to engage with should ignite your passion. Passion acts as a catalyst for perseverance; it drives you through challenges and setbacks that are inevitable in any problem-solving endeavor. When your interests align with the issues at hand, you are more likely to explore creative solutions and remain committed even when faced with obstacles. Furthermore, working on problems that excite you can lead to personal fulfillment and professional growth.

Build on Your Strengths

Identifying and leveraging your strengths is essential in effective problem-solving. Each individual possesses unique skills and talents that can be harnessed to address specific challenges. By focusing on areas where you excel, you not only increase your chances of success but also build confidence in your abilities. Moreover, engaging with problems that align with your strengths can help uncover unrecognized capabilities skills, or talents that may have been dormant until prompted by a relevant challenge.

Address Potentially Large Concerns Timely

In today's fast-paced world, timing is critical when addressing significant concerns. Problems often evolve rapidly; thus, being proactive rather than reactive can make all the difference in mitigating their effects. By identifying potentially large concerns early on, you position yourself to implement solutions before they escalate into more complex issues. This foresight not only demonstrates leadership but also contributes positively to community or organizational well-being.

Build on What Could Get Better

Every challenge presents an opportunity for improvement not just for yourself but also for the systems or processes involved in the issue at hand. Instead of viewing problems solely as obstacles, consider them as stepping stones toward better outcomes. This mindset encourages innovation and fosters an environment where continuous improvement is valued over mere maintenance of the status quo.

Avoid Reinventing the Wheel

While creativity is essential in problem-solving, it is equally important not to waste resources reinventing existing solutions unless necessary. Many challenges have already been addressed by others who may have developed effective strategies or tools that can be adapted to your needs. Learning from these established methods can save time and effort while allowing you to focus on refining rather than recreating solutions.

Learning from Others

Collaboration and learning from others' experiences are invaluable components of effective problem-solving. Engaging with peers or mentors who have faced similar challenges can provide insights that enhance your approach significantly. Sharing knowledge fosters a culture of collective intelligence where everyone benefits from each other's successes and failures.

In conclusion, tackling problems requires a blend of passion, strength identification, timely action, innovative thinking without redundancy, and collaborative learning from others' experiences all aimed at making meaningful improvements rather than simply managing existing issues.

The Success Language

Have you heard of the Tower of Babel, where people were strong and industrious before God scattered languages across the earth? This biblical narrative serves as a powerful metaphor for communication and collaboration. In ancient times, when one nation conquered another, they often imposed their language upon the defeated to ensure dominance and facilitate unity. Language was not merely a means of communication; it was a tool for power, control, and cohesion. The ability to speak the same language allowed diverse groups to come together, share ideas, and work towards common goals. This historical context highlights the importance of language in shaping societies and fostering relationships.

Today, we find ourselves on the brink of a new linguistic evolution a language that transcends mere words and embodies principles of achievement and fulfillment. I call this emerging dialect the "Success Language." Unlike conventional languages that can be learned through rote memorization or formal education, the Success Language is less understood and mastered by only a select few. It encompasses concepts such as resilience, adaptability, vision, collaboration, and emotional intelligence qualities that are essential for navigating today's complex world. You can learn this language too; it is accessible to anyone willing to invest time and effort into understanding its nuances.

Only those who can fluently speak the language of success will unlock their true-life purpose. When individuals share a common understanding of success-oriented principles, they relate better to one another and cooperate more fully than those who do not grasp these concepts. This shared lexicon fosters an environment where innovation thrives, relationships deepen, and collective aspirations are realized. Therefore, you must dedicate yourself to learning this vital language.

Understanding subject-verb agreements in this context may seem trivial at first glance; however, it symbolizes the importance of clarity in communication an essential component of success. Just as subject-verb agreement ensures grammatical accuracy in writing and speaking, mastering the fundamentals of success will help you articulate your goals clearly and pursue them with conviction. By honing your skills in this area, you will be better equipped to discover your true purpose in life.

To truly embrace the Success Language, commit yourself to continuous learning and application of what you acquire along your journey. Engage with mentors who speak this language fluently; read books that challenge your thinking; and attend workshops that push you beyond your limits. Each step taken toward understanding this language will enable you to expand beyond your current environment and leave behind the confines of your comfort zone. Remember that satisfaction often breeds complacency a state where growth stagnates. To achieve greatness requires stepping into discomfort with courage.

In conclusion, just as ancient civilizations thrived through shared languages that fostered unity and strength among their people, so too can we thrive today by embracing the Success Language. By dedicating ourselves to learning its intricacies through practice, engagement with others who share our aspirations we can unlock doors previously thought closed and embark on a journey toward realizing our fullest potential.

Did You Get the True Sense of it?

The wisest of men once said, "Wisdom is vindicated by its results." Would you not agree? This profound statement encapsulates a fundamental truth about the nature of wisdom and knowledge: their true value is revealed through their practical application and the outcomes they generate. In other words, wisdom is not merely an abstract concept or a collection of facts; it is a living force that manifests in our actions and decisions. The true test of knowledge lies in how effectively you apply it to achieve results in your life. It prompts us to reflect on our own experiences and consider whether we are truly harnessing the power of what we know.

You might ask yourself, "If the teachings in this book claim to be practical, shouldn't they produce tangible improvements in my life? How can they help me with the problems I'm facing right now?" These questions are essential for anyone seeking personal growth and transformation. They challenge us to evaluate the relevance and applicability of the information we consume. It's not enough to simply read or understand concepts; we must actively engage with them and integrate them into our daily lives. This engagement requires a commitment to action a willingness to experiment with new ideas, confront challenges head-on, and adapt our strategies based on our experiences.

Consider this example: "The span of our life is 70 years, or 80 if one is especially strong. But they are filled with trouble and sorrow; they quickly pass by, and away we fly." This poignant observation serves as a reminder of the fleeting nature of time and the importance of making every moment

> **Wisdom is vindicated by its results."**
>
> *The real test of knowing is how you make it work for you when you apply it.*
>
> *"When people speak the same language, they seem to relate better and cooperate more fully than people who do not understand the same language."*

count. Life's brevity underscores the urgency of applying what we learn without delay. We often find ourselves caught in cycles of procrastination or indecision, allowing opportunities to slip through our fingers while we ponder over theoretical knowledge instead of taking decisive action.

Therefore, put into practice what you are reading now. The principles outlined within these pages are not mere suggestions; they are actionable insights designed to propel you toward meaningful change. Like those before you who have applied the recommended solutions found in this book, tackle procrastination head-on. Embrace a proactive mindset that prioritizes implementation over contemplation. Start small if necessary, set achievable goals that align with your newfound understanding, and gradually build momentum as you witness positive changes unfold in your life.

In conclusion, wisdom indeed finds its validation through results. By actively engaging with knowledge and applying it purposefully, you can transform your understanding into tangible benefits that enhance your quality of life. Reflect on your journey thus far: Are you merely an observer of wisdom, or are you an active participant in its unfolding narrative? The choice is yours.

Procrastination

Procrastination is a pervasive issue that affects individuals across various walks of life, often leading to significant negative consequences. It is essential to recognize that delaying important tasks in favor of seemingly more enjoyable activities such as lounging around or watching television can have detrimental effects on both mental and physical well-being. This habit not only increases stress levels but also contributes to diminished performance quality in the long run.

When individuals procrastinate, they often find themselves racing against time as deadlines approach. This last-minute rush can result in sleepless nights filled with anxiety and worry, which can further exacerbate feelings of inadequacy and overwhelm. The cycle of procrastination can create a vicious loop where the initial avoidance of tasks leads to increased pressure, ultimately resulting in poorer outcomes than if the work had been completed promptly.

To combat procrastination effectively, it is crucial to adopt practical strategies that promote better time management and organization. One highly effective method is to maintain a journal or planner on your desk dedicated to scheduling upcoming tasks and responsibilities. By writing down deadlines and breaking larger projects into manageable steps, individuals can visualize their workload more clearly and prioritize their efforts accordingly. This proactive approach not only helps in managing time effectively but also fosters a sense of accomplishment as tasks are completed progressively.

Additionally, setting specific goals and establishing a routine can significantly reduce the temptation to procrastinate. Allocating designated times for work interspersed with short breaks can enhance focus and productivity while minimizing distractions. Moreover, cultivating self-discipline through consistent practice can lead to improved habits over time, making it easier to tackle tasks head-on rather than avoiding them.

Ultimately, overcoming procrastination requires a commitment to change and an understanding of its underlying causes. By recognizing the harmful impacts of this behavior and implementing structured planning techniques, individuals can reclaim control over their schedules, reduce stress levels, and achieve better performance outcomes in both personal and professional spheres.

Imagine Walking a Dark Path

Imagine walking along a dark path late one evening, enveloped by the shadows of the night. The air is cool and crisp, and the sounds of nature surround you perhaps the rustle of leaves or the distant call of an owl. Despite the sun having set long ago, casting an inky blackness over your surroundings, you're not hopelessly lost because you hold a powerful flashlight in your hand. This flashlight is more than just a tool; it symbolizes clarity and direction in times of uncertainty.

The Power of Illumination

When you point it downward, you see clearly what's immediately in front of you the uneven ground beneath your feet, the occasional rock or twig that could trip you up if you're not careful. This close-range visibility allows you to navigate safely through immediate obstacles, ensuring that each step is taken with confidence. You can appreciate the details around you: perhaps the texture of the earth or the subtle glow of bioluminescent fungi peeking through the underbrush.

However, when you point your flashlight forward, its beam cuts through the darkness and illuminates your path far into the distance. This broader perspective reveals not only where you are but also where you're headed. You can see potential forks in the road ahead, allowing you to make informed decisions about which direction to take. The light serves as a guidepost for your journey, highlighting both opportunities and challenges that lie ahead.

Choosing to Use Your Light

Will you use it? Surely, you would! The choice to utilize this illuminating tool is crucial. It provides an enlightening view of the future, enabling you to see and follow a path that leads to lasting happiness and contentment. By actively engaging with this source of light this metaphor for knowledge, insight, and foresight you empower yourself to navigate life's complexities with greater ease.

Navigating Challenges Effectively

This practical approach allows you to navigate challenges effectively and make meaningful progress toward your goals. Just as a flashlight helps illuminate physical paths in the darkness, self-awareness, and strategic planning illuminate our journeys through life's uncertainties. By understanding our strengths and weaknesses and by being aware of external factors we can chart courses that align with our values and aspirations.

In essence, using this metaphorical flashlight means embracing proactive decision-making rather than reactive responses to life's unpredictability. It encourages us to look beyond immediate concerns and consider long-term implications for our choices. With every step illuminated by this light, we gain confidence in our ability to overcome obstacles while remaining focused on our ultimate destination.

Walking along a dark path with a powerful flashlight serves as an apt metaphor for navigating life's journey. By choosing to use this light wisely both literally and figuratively we can enhance our understanding of ourselves and our environment while making informed decisions that lead us toward fulfillment and joy.

Money Relationship as a Means to an End

To effectively fill our needs and impact the lives of ourselves and others, we mustn't remain in a state of poverty. Attracting riches and abundance is not merely a matter of luck; it requires a conscious effort to cultivate a positive relationship with money. This begins with being acutely aware of our thoughts, beliefs, and opinions regarding financial matters. Negative or unhealthy discourse about money can severely undermine our chances of achieving financial success. Just as one would avoid speaking poorly about the health of our relationships, it is crucial to adopt a constructive dialogue about wealth.

Consider the analogy of a computer or mobile device infected by a virus. When your device begins to malfunction due to such an infection, your first step is to recognize that viruses are attracted to vulnerabilities within the system. The next logical step is to perform a scan and clean-up exercise, which will help restore functionality and efficiency. In this context, negative thoughts about money act similarly; they can infiltrate our mindset and create barriers that prevent us from attracting wealth. These detrimental beliefs often stem from misinformation or societal conditioning regarding finance.

Therefore, just as you would regularly maintain your electronic devices by scanning for viruses and cleaning them up, it is essential to periodically assess your mental landscape concerning money. This involves identifying any negative thought patterns or limiting beliefs that may be hindering your financial growth. Engaging in practices such as mindfulness meditation, journaling about your financial goals, or seeking out educational resources on personal finance can serve as effective methods for this mental clean-up process.

Moreover, understanding the root causes of these negative perceptions can empower you to reframe them into more constructive narratives. For instance, instead of viewing money as something scarce or inherently evil, consider it as a tool that enables you to fulfill your potential and contribute positively to society. By shifting your perspective in this way, you not only enhance your relationship with money but also open yourself up to greater opportunities for abundance.

In conclusion, cultivating a healthy relationship with money is essential for achieving financial success and impacting the lives around us positively. It requires ongoing self-awareness and proactive measures akin to maintaining our electronic devices against viruses regularly scanning our thoughts for negativity and cleaning them up so we can function optimally in our pursuit of wealth.

To truly thrive in our financial lives, it is essential to *cultivate a good relationship with money*. Wealth and abundance are not merely external circumstances; they are integral parts of our existence that influence our overall well-being. Just as we nurture our relationships by investing time, energy, and positive communication so too must we approach our finances with mindfulness and respect.

Awareness of Thoughts and Opinions about Money

Being aware of your thoughts and opinions about money is akin to maintaining a healthy dialogue in any trusted relationship. This awareness allows you to identify negative beliefs or fears that may be hindering your financial growth. For instance, if you frequently think or say things like "money is the root of all evil" or "I'll never have enough," these limiting beliefs can create a barrier between you and the abundance you seek. Instead, fostering a mindset of gratitude for what you have and an openness to receiving more can significantly shift your financial reality.

Communication with Money

Just as you would not speak thoughtlessly about someone you care for deeply; it is crucial to avoid treating money carelessly. This means being intentional in how you manage your finances budgeting wisely, investing thoughtfully, and spending consciously. When you treat money with respect, acknowledging its role in your life without fear or disdain, it becomes easier to attract wealth into your life. The energy you project towards money often reflects on your financial situation; thus, a positive attitude can lead to better opportunities and outcomes.

The Consequences of Ruthlessness

Dealing ruthlessly with money whether through reckless spending, neglecting savings, or ignoring financial education can lead to detrimental consequences. If you approach money with hostility or indifference, it may very well slip through your fingers. Financial instability often stems from a lack of understanding or appreciation for the value of money. By cultivating a respectful relationship with your finances, you're more likely to make informed decisions that promote long-term wealth accumulation rather than short-term gratification.

Building Trust with Your Finances

Trust is foundational in any relationship; similarly, building trust with your finances involves creating systems that allow for transparency and accountability. This could mean setting up regular check-ins on your budget or seeking advice from financial professionals who can guide you toward making sound investments. The more trust you build within this realm, the more secure you'll feel about taking calculated risks that can lead to greater wealth.

In conclusion, nurturing a healthy relationship with money requires ongoing effort and self-reflection. By becoming aware of your thoughts about finances, communicating positively with them, avoiding ruthlessness in dealings, and building trust through informed decision-making, you create an environment where wealth can flourish naturally.

CHAPTER 3
A PURPOSE IN LIFE

"There is more happiness in giving than there is in receiving."

The Joy of Giving: A Deeper Exploration
"There is more happiness in giving than there is in receiving." This timeless adage encapsulates a profound truth about the human experience. Reflect for a moment on your own life. Can you recall an instance when you extended a helping hand to someone in need? Perhaps it was a time when you provided material assistance, such as donating clothes to those less fortunate or contributing to a local charity. Alternatively, consider the moments when you offered emotional support, listening intently as a friend shared their struggles and vulnerabilities. In both scenarios, did you not feel overwhelming fulfillment and joy from brightening another person's day?

The Essence of Giving
This phenomenon can be attributed to humanity's intrinsic nature; we are wired for connection and compassion. When we give selflessly through tangible resources or emotional support we engage in acts that resonate deeply within our souls. These acts foster a sense of belonging and community, reinforcing our interconnectedness with others. Giving transcends mere obligation; it becomes a source of genuine happiness that enriches our lives.

The Psychological Benefits

Research in psychology supports the notion that altruistic behavior leads to increased well-being. Studies have shown that individuals who engage in acts of kindness often report higher happiness and life satisfaction levels. This phenomenon is sometimes referred to as the "helper's high," where giving triggers the release of endorphins and other feel-good hormones in our brains. This biochemical response elevates our mood and reinforces the idea that our contributions matter, enhancing our sense of purpose and self-worth.

Finding Purpose Through Generosity

Moreover, giving without expecting anything in return cultivates a profound sense of purpose. It allows us to step outside ourselves and focus on the needs and well-being of others. In doing so, we discover that our existence holds significance beyond our individual pursuits. We become part of something larger a community, a movement, or simply the shared human experience. This realization can be transformative; it instills within us an understanding that we are valuable contributors to society.

We find the greatest happiness when we give without expecting anything in return. Whether through material assistance or emotional support, these acts enrich those who receive and those who give. They satisfy our souls fundamentally, giving us purpose and affirming our importance.

The Importance of Having a Sense of Purpose

Having a sense of purpose is crucial for our overall well-being and happiness. It serves as a guiding star in the often-tumultuous journey of life, providing direction and meaning that can transform our daily experiences into something profoundly fulfilling. When we possess a clear sense of purpose, we are not merely drifting through life; we are actively engaged in pursuits that resonate with our core values and aspirations. This engagement fosters motivation, enabling us to tackle challenges with resilience and determination.

Motivation and Engagement

A well-defined purpose acts as a catalyst for motivation. It ignites our passion and drives us to invest time and energy into activities that matter to us. This heightened level of engagement enhances our productivity and enriches our experiences, making them more enjoyable and rewarding. When faced with obstacles or setbacks, individuals with a strong sense of purpose are better equipped to navigate these difficulties. They view challenges as opportunities for growth rather than insurmountable barriers, significantly contributing to their emotional resilience.

Prioritization and Accomplishment

Furthermore, having a sense of purpose allows us to prioritize our time and energy effectively. In an age where distractions abound, focusing on what truly matters becomes increasingly important. A clear purpose helps us discern between activities aligning with our goals and those not, leading to more intentional living. Each step taken toward achieving our objectives brings with it a profound sense of accomplishment and pride. These small victories accumulate over time, reinforcing our self-worth and confidence.

Connection and Community

In addition to personal benefits, a strong sense of purpose can foster connections with others who share similar values and aspirations. This shared journey creates bonds that transcend superficial interactions, cultivating a sense of belonging within communities. Engaging with like-minded individuals can provide support during challenging times, as well as opportunities for collaboration that enhance both personal growth and collective achievement.

Consequences of Lacking Purpose

Conversely, the absence of a sense of purpose can lead to feelings of disorientation or unfulfillment. Individuals may find themselves grappling with existential questions about the meaning of their lives, which can spiral into deeper emotional issues such as depression or anxiety. The struggle to find satisfaction in daily activities may result in apathy—a state where one feels disconnected from both themselves and the world around them.

In summary, having a purpose in life is essential for mental and emotional well-being. It empowers us to lead happier, more fulfilling lives by providing direction, enhancing motivation, fostering connections with others, and instilling a profound sense of accomplishment.

One Author noted,

"It is virtually impossible to give yourself away without getting back more than you give, provided you give away with no thought of any reward."

Yet, when we give of ourselves, especially to those who have no way of returning the favor, we do receive a reward. We become part of a bigger picture—an everlasting image. Helping others is like a loan to them that they might repay indirectly with interest to you or others through some kindness, which is a true hope for the future! It is what makes us human in the first place.

Pursue Your Purpose No Matter the Delayed Outcome

What happens when we start pursuing what we want? We face challenges and obstacles in our lives. Ones that were always present and never even there at all in the first place. Thus, when you set out to find your life's purpose, you will find many of these challenges trying to hold you back. But don't allow it.

Don't let fear stop you from doing what you want, no matter the Outcome.

I'm very passionate about guiding people out of their inner fear. That's why I recently experienced one of the proudest, most exciting, and most terrifying moments of my life when I ventured into this writing goal.

Overcoming Negative Self-Talk: A Path to Empowerment

Now, there may be a voice in your head saying you don't deserve something or aren't ready. Perhaps it whispers that you lack the time or energy to pursue your dreams and aspirations. This internal dialogue is not unique to you; it's a common experience shared by many individuals across various walks of life. These negative voices can manifest as self-doubt, fear of failure, or feelings of inadequacy, often hindering our ability to take action toward our goals.

So, Break Yourself Free!

While it may seem daunting, breaking free from these negative beliefs is not only possible but essential for personal growth and fulfillment. It's important to recognize that you cannot entirely silence these negative voices—no matter how hard you strive to maintain an optimistic outlook on your purpose. However, you can actively challenge and replace these detrimental thoughts with empowering affirmations that bolster your confidence and resilience.

The journey of breaking free from negative beliefs can be both challenging and rewarding. The moment you embark on the path toward realizing your purpose, it becomes imperative to liberate yourself from the shackles of negativity. Start by identifying the specific negative beliefs that plague your mind. This requires introspection and honesty with yourself; take note of the recurring thoughts that undermine your self-worth or potential.

Once pinpointing these limiting beliefs, the next step is to confront them head-on. Ask yourself whether these thoughts are based on facts or merely perceptions shaped by past experiences or societal expectations. Often, you'll find that these negative narratives are unfounded and do not reflect your true capabilities or worthiness.

After challenging these beliefs, replace them with positive affirmations—statements reinforcing your strengths and potential. For instance, instead of thinking, "I don't deserve success," reframe this thought into "I am worthy of success and capable of achieving my goals." By consistently practicing this reframing technique, you gradually rewire your brain to adopt a more empowering mindset. The first step in breaking free from negative beliefs is to identify them. This may involve taking time to reflect on your thoughts and behaviors and identifying patterns of negativity. Ask yourself if there is evidence to support these beliefs or if they are based on assumptions or past experiences. Try to reframe these beliefs more positively and realistically. Not only will it clear things for you, but it will allow you to practice positive self-talk.

Negative beliefs often lead to negative self-talk. To break free from these beliefs, you should practice positive self-talk. Focus on your strengths and accomplishments, and use affirmations to reinforce positive beliefs about yourself. Additionally, surrounding yourself with supportive individuals who uplift and encourage you can significantly impact your journey toward self-empowerment. Seek out friends, family members, or colleagues who are supportive, optimistic, and encouraging.

Engage in communities or relationships where positivity thrives; this will help reinforce the new beliefs you're cultivating within yourself.

Understanding the Need for Professional Help in Overcoming Negative Thoughts and Beliefs

When it becomes exceedingly challenging to break free from the grip of negative thoughts and entrenched beliefs, it is crucial to consider seeking professional help. Negative beliefs, manifesting as persistent self-doubt, pessimism, or a distorted view of reality, can significantly hinder personal growth and overall well-being. If these detrimental thought patterns affect your daily life-impacting relationships, work performance, or emotional health, then reaching out for professional assistance is not just advisable but essential.

A qualified therapist or counselor can provide a safe and supportive environment where you can explore these negative beliefs without judgment. They possess the expertise to help you identify the root causes of your negative thinking and guide you through reframing these thoughts into more constructive perspectives. You can learn effective coping strategies tailored to your unique situation through various therapeutic approaches—such as Cognitive Behavioral Therapy (CBT), mindfulness practices, or narrative therapy.

Moreover, engaging with a mental health professional allows you to develop practical techniques that empower you to challenge and dismantle harmful beliefs. This might include exercises in cognitive restructuring, where you actively question the validity of your negative thoughts, or practicing mindfulness meditation to cultivate greater awareness of your thought patterns. These strategies not only assist in breaking free from negativity but foster resilience and promote a more positive outlook on life.

If negative beliefs significantly impact your life, seeking professional help is imperative. A therapist or counselor can equip you with the tools and insights to navigate these challenges effectively. Investing in your mental health through professional guidance opens the door to personal transformation and a brighter future.

In conclusion, while the journey may be fraught with challenges, breaking free from negative beliefs opens up possibilities for personal growth and fulfillment. Embrace this transformative process with patience and determination as you work towards creating the life you've always envisioned for yourself.

Do You Have All the Facts?

In my book, "Result Beyond the Finish Line," I aim to dismantle the pervasive myths surrounding money that often cloud our judgment and hinder our financial growth. Common beliefs such as "You need to own real estate," "You should cut back on sleep," "Money does not grow on trees," "You must work extra hard," or "You have to be lucky" are ingrained in our societal mindset. But do you truly accept everything you hear without question? The reality is that a significant amount of misinformation exists, and one of my primary objectives in this book is to guide you toward understanding what it genuinely takes to live your life purposefully by critically evaluating the information presented to you.

In an age where we are inundated with information from countless sources—social media, news outlets, blogs, and more it becomes increasingly crucial for us to develop the skills necessary to assess this information effectively. Without these skills, we risk allowing misleading narratives to shape our thoughts and decisions. We must gather reliable facts to arrive at accurate conclusions about money and success. This process involves discerning credible sources from those that propagate falsehoods or half-truths.

Moreover, it's essential to recognize that not all advice is created equal; what works for one person may not necessarily apply to another. Therefore, cultivating a mindset of inquiry and skepticism can empower you to sift through the noise and identify strategies that align with your unique circumstances and aspirations. Doing so allows you to break free from limiting beliefs and embrace a more informed perspective on wealth creation and personal fulfillment. It also helps us to avoid falling prey to misinformation, propaganda, and fake news, which can have serious real-world consequences. Furthermore, critical thinking and information evaluation skills are essential for success in many professions and being an engaged and informed member of society. By developing these skills, we can learn to be more discerning information consumers and make better decisions based on accurate and reliable information.

Ultimately, I hope that "Result Beyond the Finish Line" catalyzes your journey toward financial literacy and self-discovery. It encourages readers to question conventional wisdom and seek out factual information that resonates with their individual goals. In doing so, we can collectively challenge outdated paradigms about money and redefine what it means to achieve true success in our lives.

Do You Really Believe Every Word? The Information Overload of Today

In the contemporary landscape, we find ourselves inundated with an overwhelming torrent of information flowing in from many sources. This deluge comes from the vast expanse of the Internet and traditional media such as television, newspapers, and books. Additionally, our personal communications e-mails, text messages, or conversations with friends contribute significantly to this incessant data flow. The sheer volume can be staggering; sometimes, it feels as though there is no respite from the constant barrage of information vying for our attention.

Given this reality, we must exercise discernment and caution in how we consume and interpret this information. While many individuals in our social circles share insights and stories with good intentions, we must remain vigilant against the darker side of information dissemination. Some intentionally propagate misinformation or manipulate facts to serve their own agendas. This reality underscores the importance of critical thinking and skepticism in our approach to information.

We do not wish to fall into the trap of naivety by accepting every claim at face value; instead, we aspire to cultivate a mindset that encourages us to be shrewd information consumers. This involves taking a moment to ponder each piece of information before accepting it as truth. We can navigate this complex landscape more effectively by questioning its source, verifying its accuracy, and considering its context. In doing so, we empower ourselves to make informed decisions based on reliable data rather than being swayed by misleading narratives or sensationalized claims.

In an age where misinformation can spread like wildfire across social media platforms and other channels, fostering a culture of critical inquiry is essential. We must strive not only to seek out credible sources but also to engage in thoughtful discussions that challenge assumptions and promote understanding. By adopting such an approach, we can better equip ourselves to thrive amidst the chaos of modern information overload.

"Don't believe everything you hear and only half of what you see."

The Importance of Reliable Information in Decision-Making

We must rely on trustworthy and accurate facts to make sound and informed decisions. In an age where information is abundant yet often misleading, we must exercise discernment in our reading choices. This means being vigilant about the sources from which we gather information. Engaging with unreliable Internet news sites or succumbing to the allure of sensationalized e-mails that propagate rumors can lead us to misinformation. Such distractions waste our time and can cloud our judgment, leading to decisions based on false premises.

Moreover, being wary of get-rich-quick schemes and tactics that promise immediate financial gain without a solid foundation or proven methodology is crucial. These schemes often prey on individuals' desires for quick success, luring them into traps that can result in significant losses rather than the anticipated rewards. The allure of easy money can overshadow critical thinking, causing individuals to overlook the risks involved.

Unreliable information invariably leads to poor decision-making outcomes. It is a common misconception to believe that false information will not have a personal impact; however, this could not be further from the truth. Individuals who lack experience or critical analytical skills may place undue trust in every piece of information they encounter, failing to question its validity or source. This blind faith can result in misguided choices that affect various aspects of life—financially, socially, and emotionally.

In conclusion, cultivating a habit of seeking credible sources and verifying information before acting upon it is essential for effective decision-making. By prioritizing reliable facts over sensationalism and rumor, we empower ourselves to make informed choices that align with our goals and values.

Take the Small Steps

Do you like to send e-mails and text messages to your friends? When you see an exciting story in the news or hear about a unique experience, do you feel like a news reporter who wants to share it immediately? Before sending the e-mail or text, ask yourself: Am I sure this story is true? Do I really have the facts? If you are not sure, do not send it. Delete it!

Yes, start by taking small steps—one step at a time.

How can we avoid disaster? By refusing to spread harmful or unconfirmed stories and do not believe everything we hear. Instead, ensure you have the facts through testimonies and proven techniques. There may come a time when we are hurt because people spread stories about us that are only partly true. But what if someone spreads lies about you? Refrain from using all of your time trying to convince people that the stories are false.

We should only spend some time trying to convince people that the stories are false because it is ultimately a waste of time and energy. People may have already formed their opinions and beliefs about the stories, and it may be difficult to change their minds. Focusing solely on disproving the stories can also give them more attention and publicity, which may not be desired. Instead, it may be more effective to focus on promoting and highlighting the truth and bringing attention to credible sources of information. This can shift the narrative and promote accurate information.

Instead, encourage people to look at the facts (facts finding). True, wisdom is vindicated by its work. Live your life in a way that will show others who you are because our good conduct will disprove any half-truths and false accusations against us. You will come to complete this book sooner or later since you are the kind of person who is constantly looking for more.

Do Not Rely on Yourself

In our journey through life, we must recognize that relying solely on our insights and experiences can lead us astray. While personal wisdom gained from years of schooling and life experiences can be invaluable, it often comes with inherent limitations. Over time, we may develop a sense of self-assuredness that borders on arrogance, believing our understanding of the world is comprehensive and infallible. This mindset can create a dangerous illusion; we might start interpreting situations through a narrow lens shaped by our biases, emotions, and preconceived notions.

As we navigate complex scenarios—whether in personal relationships, professional environments, or broader societal issues—we must remain vigilant against the temptation to assume we have all the answers. The danger lies in becoming overly confident in our interpretations and judgments without seeking additional perspectives or information. This overconfidence can cloud our judgment and prevent us from seeing the whole picture.

It is crucial to actively engage with others and seek diverse viewpoints to combat this tendency. Collaboration fosters a richer understanding of any situation by incorporating various insights that challenge our assumptions. Conducting thorough research is equally essential; gathering facts from credible sources allows us to ground our opinions in reality rather than conjecture. By consulting with others—friends, colleagues, or experts—we open ourselves up to new ideas and constructive criticism that can enhance our understanding.

In conclusion, while self-reliance has merits, it is vital to balance it with humility and openness to external input. Embracing collaboration and diligent research enriches our knowledge and helps us make more informed decisions. Therefore, let us commit to stepping outside our comfort zones and engaging meaningfully with the world around us.

> *"When anyone replies to a matter before he hears the facts, it is foolish and humiliating."*

The Importance of Open-Mindedness in Evaluating Situations

In our daily interactions and evaluations of various situations, adopting a mindset that encourages open-mindedness and critical thinking is crucial. It can also become challenging to evaluate a situation correctly if we do not widen out by thinking outside the box or when we prejudice a person (or a specific group we don't feel comfortable with). This narrow perspective can lead us to form judgments based on preconceived notions rather than objective analysis. When we allow our biases to dictate our perceptions, we risk fostering an environment of suspicion and mistrust toward those around us.

For instance, if we focus excessively on our cultural, social, or ideological differences, we may inadvertently cultivate an atmosphere of wariness toward our neighbors. We may become suspicious of our neighbors if we keep thinking about our differences. This suspicion can be exacerbated by external influences, such as negative rumors or stereotypes circulating within our communities. Consequently, when we hear something unfavorable about someone from a different background or belief system, then if we hear something negative about him/her, we may want to believe it, even if there is no proof that it is true. This tendency to accept unverified information as truth underscores the importance of questioning the validity of what we hear and challenging our biases.

This phenomenon serves as a poignant reminder of negative feelings' power over our judgment. This is a very important lesson for us; if we allow ourselves to have negative feelings about people, it can cause us to reach wrong conclusions that are not based on facts and even blur our opportunities. By succumbing to these emotions and allowing them to cloud our judgment, we not only misinterpret the intentions and actions of others but also potentially miss out on valuable opportunities for connection and collaboration.

To counteract this tendency, it is essential that we actively work towards broadening our perspectives through empathy and understanding. Engaging with diverse viewpoints allows us to challenge our assumptions and fosters a more inclusive environment where constructive dialogue can thrive. Doing so empowers us to make more informed decisions grounded in reality rather than fear or prejudice.

In conclusion, cultivating an open-minded approach is vital for accurate evaluation. It enables us to transcend superficial differences and fosters healthier community relationships.

Widen Your Perspective

Allowing ourselves to have negative feelings about people can have several negative consequences. It can cause us to reach wrong conclusions that are not based on facts. When we have negative feelings towards someone, we are more likely to interpret their actions and behaviors in a negative light, even if there is no evidence to support our assumptions. This can lead to misunderstandings, conflicts, and damaged relationships.

It is crucial to adopt a mindset that encourages open-mindedness and critical thinking. It can also become challenging to evaluate a situation correctly if we do not widen out by thinking outside the box or when we prejudice a person (or a particular group we don't feel comfortable with). This narrow perspective can lead us to form judgments based on preconceived notions rather than objective analysis. When we allow our biases to dictate our perceptions, we risk fostering an environment of suspicion and mistrust toward those around us.

For instance, if we focus excessively on our cultural, social, or ideological differences, we may inadvertently cultivate an atmosphere of wariness toward our neighbors. We may become suspicious of our neighbors if we keep thinking about our differences. This suspicion can be exacerbated by external influences, such as negative rumors or stereotypes circulating within our communities. Consequently, when we hear something unfavorable about someone from a different background or belief system, then if we hear something negative about him/her, we may want to believe it, even if there is no proof that it is true. This tendency to accept unverified information as truth underscores the importance of questioning the validity of what we hear and challenging our biases.

This phenomenon serves as a poignant reminder of negative feelings' power over our judgment. This is a very important lesson for us; if we allow ourselves to have negative feelings about people, it can cause us to reach wrong conclusions that are not based on facts and even blur our opportunities. By succumbing to these emotions and allowing them to cloud our judgment, we not only misinterpret the intentions and actions of others but also potentially miss out on valuable opportunities for connection and collaboration.

To counteract this tendency, it is essential that we actively work towards broadening our perspectives through empathy and understanding. Engaging with diverse viewpoints allows us to challenge our assumptions and fosters a more inclusive environment where constructive dialogue can thrive. Doing so empowers us to make more informed decisions grounded in reality rather than fear or prejudice.

Furthermore, negative feelings can also blur our opportunities. When we have negative feelings towards someone, we may unconsciously avoid interacting with them or seeking collaboration opportunities. This can limit our professional and personal growth, as we may miss out on valuable insights, experiences, and connections that could help us achieve our goals.

In short, allowing ourselves to have negative feelings about people can harm our relationships, opportunities, and overall well-being. It is essential to recognize and challenge our negative biases and strive to approach others with an open mind and a willingness to learn and grow. In conclusion, cultivating an open-minded approach is vital for accurate evaluation. It enables us to transcend superficial differences and fosters healthier community relationships.

Can Anything Good Come Out of Nazarene?

In our complex human experience, we often navigate a landscape rife with judgment and preconceived notions. Living in a world steeped in prejudice, we tend to evaluate people and situations based on superficial observations or societal narratives that shape our beliefs. We unconsciously construct opinions about others daily, influenced by what we hear, see, or are conditioned to believe. This tendency to judge can cloud our understanding and prevent us from recognizing the potential for goodness, even in the most unlikely places.

Now, let's consider a hypothetical scenario that challenges this instinctive judgment: Imagine walking along a darkened path when suddenly you hear an unfamiliar voice urging you to step aside immediately because a speeding train is barreling toward you. In that crisis, would you pause to question the voice's identity or credibility? Most likely not. Your survival instinct would kick in; your immediate response would be to heed the warning and move out of harm's way without hesitation. This example is a powerful metaphor for overlooking critical insights simply because they come from unexpected sources.

The essence of this narrative invites us to reflect on the broader implications of our judgments. Just as that strange voice could be a harbinger of safety in a life-threatening situation, so too can seemingly unremarkable origins yield profound outcomes. This book, "Results Beyond the Finished Line," beautifully demonstrates this idea, suggesting that what may initially appear unworthy or insignificant can lead to extraordinary results if given a chance.

In conclusion, while dismissing something based on preconceived notions or societal biases is easy, it is crucial to remain open-minded and receptive to possibilities that challenge our assumptions. The potential for good can emerge from anywhere, even from places like Nazarene—if we allow ourselves the grace of exploration rather than judgment.

CHAPTER 4
FIVE (5) IMPORTANT LIFE MANAGEMENT QUESTIONS TO ANSWER

1. What?

What do you want to do with your life? This is probably one of the most important questions you will ever answer. The answer to this question will lay the foundation for your destiny. Once you have clearly identified what you want to do with your life, it then becomes the focal point of everything you plan to do. Knowing what you want to do gives you clarity and a much-needed sense of purpose. It also prevents you from engaging in side-tracking, time-wasting ventures which have no connection to your purpose. There are 5 steps that will help us answer the question – What!

Step 1: Self-Reflection

Begin by engaging in self-reflection. Take time to think about your interests, values, strengths, and passions. Consider the activities that bring you joy and fulfillment. Journaling can be an effective tool for this process; write down your thoughts, feelings, and experiences that resonate with you.

Step 2: Identify Your Values

Understanding what matters most to you is crucial in determining your life's direction. Values such as family, career success, creativity, adventure, or community service can guide your decisions. Make a list of your core values and rank them in order of importance.

Step 3: Explore Your Passions

Passions are the things that excite you and make you feel alive. Think about hobbies or subjects that captivate your attention. Ask yourself questions like:

- What activities make me lose track of time?
- What topics could I talk about endlessly?
- What issues in the world do I feel strongly about?

Step 4: Set Goals

Once you've identified your values and passions, translate them into specific goals. These goals should be SMART (Specific, Measurable, Achievable, Relevant, Time-bound). For example:

- Instead of saying, "I want to help people," specify, "I want to become a licensed counselor within five years."

Step 5: Research Opportunities

Investigate various paths that align with your identified goals. This could involve exploring different careers, educational programs, volunteer opportunities, or entrepreneurial ventures. Networking with professionals in fields of interest can provide valuable insights.

Step 6: Create an Action Plan

Develop a detailed action plan outlining the steps needed to achieve your goals. Break down larger objectives into smaller tasks with deadlines to maintain momentum.

Step 7: Stay Flexible

Life is unpredictable; therefore, it's essential to remain adaptable as circumstances change. Be open to reassessing your goals and making adjustments along the way.

Ultimately, knowing what you want to do with your life provides clarity and purpose. It serves as a compass guiding all aspects of decision-making and prioritization in both personal and professional realms. By following these steps—self-reflection, identifying values and passions, setting goals, researching opportunities, creating an action plan, and staying flexible—you can carve out a meaningful path that resonates deeply with the results you set up to achieve.

2. Why

The second question is why? Understanding the importance of why you want to achieve certain things in your life is the motivation that will drive you to accomplish the goals that you have set for yourself. Why do you want to achieve these goals you have set for yourself? For example, why do you want to lose weight? Why do you want to get married? Why do you want to start your own business? Why do you want to boost your self-esteem? The answers to these questions must be compelling enough to move you to take action, which will serve as your motivation. This intrinsic motivation serves as a driving force that propels you toward your objectives. Also, understanding why you want to achieve something makes it easier to stay committed and focused, especially when faced with challenges or setbacks. Let's explore this concept step by step, using various examples to illustrate how identifying your motivations can lead to successful goal attainment.

Examples of Goals and Their Underlying Motivations

a. Losing Weight

- Why do you want to lose weight?
  - The desire to lose weight often stems from multiple motivations: health concerns (such as reducing the risk of chronic diseases), improving physical appearance (which can enhance self-esteem), or increasing energy levels for daily activities.
  - Compelling Reason: A compelling reason might be wanting to live longer for your family or being able to participate in activities with friends without feeling fatigued.

b. Getting Married

- Why do you want to get married?
  - Marriage may represent a commitment to love and partnership, social acceptance, or the desire for family stability.
  - oCompelling Reason: A strong motivation could be the wish for emotional support through life's ups and downs or the aspiration to build a family together.

c. Starting Your Own Business

- Why do you want to start your own business?
  - This goal might be driven by aspirations for financial independence, the desire for creative freedom, or dissatisfaction with traditional employment.
  - Compelling Reason: A powerful motivation could be wanting to create something meaningful that aligns with personal values or making a positive impact on society.

d. Boosting Self-Esteem

- Why do you want to boost your self-esteem?
    - Higher self-esteem can lead to better mental health, improved relationships, and greater success in various life areas.
    - Compelling Reason: A motivating factor might be overcoming past traumas or negative experiences that have hindered personal growth and happiness.

Crafting Your Personal "Why" Statement

Once you've identified your motivations for each goal, it's beneficial to articulate them clearly. This can take the form of a personal "why" statement that encapsulates what drives you:

- For example: "I want to lose weight because I want to feel confident in my body and enjoy an active lifestyle with my children."

The Impact of Understanding Your "Why"

Recognizing your motivations not only helps clarify your goals but also enhances resilience against obstacles. When challenges arise—and they will—you can refer back to your compelling reasons as reminders of why you embarked on this journey in the first place.

Therefore, understanding why you want to achieve certain things in life is fundamental for effective life management. It transforms vague aspirations into actionable goals fueled by passion and purpose. By reflecting on these motivations regularly, you reinforce your commitment and increase your likelihood of success.

3. Who?

For you to achieve certain results, you need to take on certain qualities. Who do you need to become as you strive to achieve your goal? Do you need to become more confident, committed, and action-oriented? Do you need to become a risk-taker? Do you need to be more assertive? Identify the qualities that you need to adopt to achieve your goals. Max Dupree rightly said, "We cannot become what we need to be, by remaining what we are." Therefore, to effectively achieve your goals, it is essential to reflect on the qualities you need to cultivate within yourself. This process involves a deep understanding of who you are currently and who you aspire to become. Here is a comprehensive breakdown of the qualities that may be necessary for personal growth and goal attainment.

1. Self-Confidence

Self-confidence is foundational in pursuing any goal. It allows you to trust in your abilities and judgments, which can lead to taking decisive actions. To develop this quality, consider engaging in activities that challenge your comfort zone, seeking feedback from trusted peers, and celebrating small victories along the way.

2. Commitment

Commitment refers to the dedication and perseverance required to see your goals through to completion. This quality often involves setting clear intentions and being willing to put in the necessary effort over time. To enhance your commitment, create a structured plan with milestones that keep you accountable and motivated.

3. Action Orientation

Being action-oriented means prioritizing action over procrastination or indecision. This quality encourages you to take initiative rather than waiting for the perfect moment or conditions. To foster an action-oriented mindset, practice breaking down larger tasks into manageable steps and set deadlines for each step.

4. Risk-Taking

Embracing risk-taking can be crucial when striving for significant achievements. It involves stepping outside your comfort zone and being open to new experiences, even if they come with uncertainties. To become more comfortable with risk-taking, start by assessing potential risks versus rewards in various situations and gradually expose yourself to new challenges.

5. Assertiveness

Assertiveness is about expressing your thoughts, feelings, and needs openly while respecting others' rights as well. Developing assertiveness can help you advocate for yourself in both personal and professional contexts. You can enhance this quality by practicing clear communication techniques, learning how to say no when necessary, and standing firm on your values.

6. Adaptability

In a constantly changing world, being adaptable is vital for success. This quality enables you to adjust your strategies as circumstances evolve without losing sight of your goals. To improve adaptability, embrace change as an opportunity for growth rather than a setback; seek out diverse experiences that challenge your usual ways of thinking.

7. Emotional Intelligence

Having high emotional intelligence (EI) allows you to understand and manage not only your emotions but also those of others around you. This skill can enhance interpersonal relationships and facilitate better teamwork toward achieving common goals. You can develop EI by practicing empathy—actively listening to others—and reflecting on how emotions influence decision-making.

8. Resilience

Finally, cultivating resilience equips you with the ability to bounce back from setbacks or failures encountered along the journey toward achieving your goals. Building resilience involves maintaining a positive outlook during tough times and developing coping strategies such as mindfulness or stress management techniques. In summary, becoming who you need to be requires the intentional development of these qualities: self-confidence, commitment, action orientation, risk-taking ability, assertiveness, adaptability, emotional intelligence, and resilience. As Max Dupree stated: "We cannot become what we need to be by remaining what we are." By actively working on these attributes, you'll position yourself more favorably toward achieving your desired outcomes.

4. The How?

Achieving results in life management requires a structured approach that encompasses clear objectives, actionable steps, and the flexibility to adapt when necessary.

Let's see a comprehensive guide on how to effectively manage your life goals, using weight loss as an illustrative example.

1. Define Clear Objectives

The first step in achieving any goal is to define what you want to achieve clearly. For weight loss, this could mean specifying how much weight you want to lose and within what timeframe.

- Example Objective: Lose 20 pounds in 4 months.

Create a Step-by-Step Plan

Once your objectives are defined, it's essential to create a detailed plan that outlines the steps needed to reach your goal.

Step 1: Research and Education

- Understand the basics of nutrition and exercise.
- Consult with healthcare professionals or registered dietitians for personalized advice.

Step 2: Set Up a Nutrition Plan

- Calculate daily caloric needs based on age, gender, and activity level.
- Develop a balanced meal plan focusing on whole foods (fruits, vegetables, lean proteins).

Step 3: Establish an Exercise Routine

- Choose activities you enjoy (e.g., walking, cycling, swimming).
- Aim for at least 150 minutes of moderate aerobic activity per week combined with strength training exercises twice a week.

Step 4: Track Progress

- Use tools like food diaries or apps (e.g., MyFitnessPal) to monitor calorie intake and exercise.
- Weigh yourself weekly and adjust your plan as necessary.

2. Implement Tools for Success

Having the right tools can significantly enhance your ability to stay organized and motivated throughout your journey.

- Apps: Utilize fitness tracking apps that help log meals and workouts.
- Support Systems: Join support groups or find workout buddies who share similar goals.
- Journals: Keep a journal for reflections on progress and emotional responses related to food and exercise.

3. Monitor and Adjust Your Plan

Regularly reviewing your progress is crucial. If you notice that you're not losing weight as expected:

- Analyze dietary habits and physical activity levels.
- Consider consulting with professionals again for further insights.

5. Prepare for Contingencies

It's important to have alternative plans ready in case your initial strategy doesn't yield the desired results.

- Plan A: Follow the original nutrition and exercise plan strictly.

If Plan A fails:

- Plan B:
  - Reassess caloric intake; consider reducing calories further if safe.
  - Change up the exercise routine—try new classes or increase intensity.
  - Seek professional guidance if self-management proves challenging.

6. Stay Motivated

Maintaining motivation over time can be difficult but is essential for long-term success:

- Set smaller milestones along the way (e.g., losing the first five pounds).
- Reward yourself for achievements with non-food-related rewards (e.g., new workout gear).

Remember, that achieving results involves setting clear objectives, creating structured plans with actionable steps, utilizing appropriate tools, monitoring progress regularly, preparing contingency plans, and maintaining motivation throughout the process. This systematic approach not only helps in achieving specific goals like weight loss but can also be applied across various areas of life management

5. The When?

Understanding the Importance of Timelines in Goal Setting will help you define the when!

However, merely setting goals without a clear timeline can lead to procrastination and lack of accountability. To ensure that your plans materialize into tangible results, it is crucial to establish when you intend to achieve your goals.

1. Defining Your Goals Clearly

Before you can determine when you will accomplish your goals, it's essential to define them clearly. This involves:

- Specificity: Make sure your goal is specific and well-defined. Instead of saying, "I want to get fit," specify, "I want to lose 10 pounds."
- Measurable Outcomes: Establish criteria for measuring progress. For example, track your weight weekly or monitor your workout frequency.
- Achievable Targets: Ensure that your goal is realistic given your current circumstances and resources.
- Relevance: Your goal should align with broader life objectives or values.
- Time-bound: This is where the timeline comes into play; every goal should have a deadline.

2. Establishing a Timeline

Once you have defined your goals, the next step is to establish a timeline:

- Set Deadlines: Decide on a specific date by which you want to achieve each goal. For instance, if you're aiming to lose 10 pounds, set a deadline of three months from today.
- Break Down Goals into Milestones: Divide larger goals into smaller milestones with their own deadlines. This makes the process less overwhelming and allows for regular assessment of progress.

- Prioritize Tasks: Determine which tasks are most critical for achieving each milestone and allocate time accordingly.

3. Taking Action

With clear goals and timelines established, it's time to take action:

- Create an Action Plan: Outline the steps needed to reach each milestone and ultimately achieve your goal.
- Start Today: The most important part of turning plans into action is starting immediately. Whether it's dedicating 30 minutes today to exercise or researching resources for a project, taking that first step is crucial.
- Stay Committed: Consistency is key in maintaining momentum toward achieving your goals within the set timelines.

4. Monitoring Progress

Regularly review your progress against the timelines you've set:

- Weekly Check-ins: Assess what you've accomplished each week relative to your milestones.
- Adjust as Necessary: If you find that you're falling behind schedule, reassess your plan and make necessary adjustments without losing sight of the goal.

5. Celebrating Achievements

Once you reach a milestone or complete a goal:

- Acknowledge Your Successes: Take time to celebrate achievements, no matter how small they may seem.
- Reflect on Lessons Learned: Consider what worked well and what could be improved for future goal-setting endeavors.

In summary, establishing when you will accomplish specific goals involves defining those goals clearly, setting realistic timelines with milestones, taking immediate action towards them, monitoring progress regularly, and celebrating achievements along the way.

By committing yourself to this structured approach, you can transform plans into reality effectively.

CHAPTER 5
CHANGING CIRCUMSTANCES

Life is inherently unpredictable, and at times, we find ourselves grappling with profound changes that can feel overwhelming. Whether it's the onset of a chronic illness, the emotional turmoil of a divorce, or the heart-wrenching loss of a loved one, these experiences can drastically alter our daily lives and mental landscapes. In such moments, it is common to feel as though you are trapped in a situation that you cannot escape from; longing for the days when life felt manageable and familiar. However, while it may seem easier to dwell on despair and reminisce about what once was, there exists an alternative path—one that involves actively seeking ways to regain control over your life.

Regaining Control

The first step towards reclaiming your sense of action and urgency is to shift your focus from what you have lost to what you can still do. This requires a conscious decision to move away from passive waiting for circumstances to improve on their own. Instead of hoping for divine intervention or wishing for a return to normalcy, consider taking proactive steps toward creating a new reality that accommodates your current situation.

Creating a New Routine

Establishing a new routine is crucial in this process. A routine provides structure and predictability in times of chaos. Begin by identifying what aspects of your life are most important to you—these could be relationships, hobbies, self-care practices, or professional goals. Prioritize these elements as you design your new daily schedule.

When crafting this schedule, take into account your current limitations and abilities. It's essential to be realistic about what you can accomplish given your circumstances; this might mean breaking tasks down into smaller, more manageable steps or allowing yourself extra time for activities that may take longer than they used to. By doing so, you create an environment where success feels attainable rather than overwhelming.

Finding Balance

In addition to prioritizing tasks based on importance, consider incorporating flexibility into your routine. Life's unpredictability means that some days will be better than others; having the ability to adjust your plans accordingly can alleviate feelings of frustration when things don't go as expected. Allow yourself grace during this transition period—acknowledge that it's okay not to have everything figured out immediately.

Building Support Networks

Another vital aspect of regaining control is reaching out for support. Surround yourself with friends and family who understand what you're going through and can offer encouragement or assistance when needed. Engaging with support groups—whether in-person or online—can also provide valuable perspectives from those who have faced similar challenges.

While it is true that changing circumstances can feel disorienting and painful, they also present an opportunity for growth and resilience. By focusing on actionable steps rather than despairing over loss, creating structured routines tailored to your current abilities, remaining flexible in the face of unpredictability, and building supportive networks around yourself, you can navigate through life's upheavals with renewed strength and purpose.

Have you become discouraged?

When faced with adversity, it is not uncommon to feel overwhelmed and disheartened. "When you become discouraged in times of distress, your power will be scanty. In other words, when you become discouraged in times of trouble, your strength will be meager." This statement sums up a profound truth about human experience: our mindset significantly influences our ability to navigate challenges. The implication here is clear: Attitude Makes a Difference.

Individuals who allow themselves to succumb to a negative mindset during difficult times often find that they relinquish the little control they still possess over their circumstances. This surrender can manifest as feelings of helplessness and despair, which only serve to exacerbate the situation. On the other hand, those who cultivate a positive outlook are more likely to tap into an inner reservoir of strength and resilience. They can summon the courage and determination needed to regain control over their lives, effectively putting themselves back in the driver's seat.

It is essential to recognize that while we may not have immediate power over our external circumstances, we do have agency over our responses to them. Our reactions can either empower us or further entrench us in negativity. By consciously choosing how we respond—whether through optimism, problem-solving, or seeking support—we can influence our trajectory toward recovery and success.

Moreover, it is crucial to acknowledge that there will inevitably be challenges along the way as we strive toward our goals. The journey toward achieving results often resembles a marathon rather than a sprint; it requires endurance and perseverance. Each obstacle encountered serves as an opportunity for growth and learning, reinforcing the idea that setbacks do not define us but rather shape our character.

Bottom Line: You may not be able to change your circumstances immediately, but you can control your responses to them. Embracing this perspective empowers you to navigate through difficulties with resilience and hope. Remember that there will be challenges along the way as you move towards your results beyond the finished line; however, maintaining a positive attitude can transform these challenges into stepping stones toward success.

The Struggle with Overwhelming Demands of Life

In today's fast-paced world, the demands of life can feel insurmountable. The children need your attention now, their innocent voices calling for guidance and support as they navigate their own challenges. Simultaneously, your employer is expecting you to meet deadlines and deliver results, adding pressure to an already full plate. On top of that, your spouse is reaching out for connection and understanding while you are also trying to care for your ailing parent, who requires both physical and emotional support. This chaotic blend of responsibilities can lead to feelings of being overwhelmed, leaving you questioning: "What can I do?" It's a common sentiment echoed by many who find themselves stretched thin by the expectations placed upon them.

This is not the life you envisioned; instead, it feels like a relentless cycle that consumes you every day. You may find yourself torn between competing priorities, feeling guilty when you cannot meet everyone's needs. The internal dialogue often revolves around the notion that "people need me!" However, responding to every demand without considering your own well-being may not be in anyone's best interests—neither yours nor those who depend on you. Recognizing this reality is the first step toward regaining control over your life.

To navigate this overwhelming landscape, it becomes essential to implement strategies that allow for balance and self-care. Since it is impossible to stand up for everyone simultaneously and ensure their satisfaction, delegating some responsibilities to family members or associates can alleviate some of the burdens. This act of sharing duties not only lightens your load but also empowers others to contribute meaningfully to the family dynamic or workplace environment.

- Taking one day at a time is another crucial approach to managing stress effectively. By breaking down tasks into manageable segments and avoiding procrastination, you create a sense of accomplishment that can motivate you further. Establishing daily routines that prioritize essential tasks while allowing flexibility can help maintain focus amidst chaos. Keep track of the number of demands you face in a week. Can any of them be delegated to others?
- Be selective about accepting social invitations. If you cannot attend because of a lack of time or energy, kindly say so.

Moreover, being open about your situation with friends, family, or colleagues can lead to unexpected support. When people understand what you're going through, they may help or simply lend an empathetic ear—both invaluable resources during challenging times.

Incorporating small moments of joy into your daily routine can also make a significant difference in how you cope with overwhelming demands. Taking just a little time each morning for activities such as gardening or engaging in light exercise provides not only physical benefits but also mental clarity and emotional satisfaction. These moments serve as reminders that amidst life's chaos, nurturing yourself is equally important.

Ultimately, regaining control over your life amid overwhelming demands requires a combination of delegation, prioritization, open communication, and self-care practices. By recognizing that it's okay not to meet every demand perfectly and by taking proactive steps towards managing stressors effectively, you pave the way for a more balanced existence where both personal fulfillment and responsibilities coexist harmoniously.

Bottom Line: If you try to do everything, you may render yourself unable to do anything.

If possible, seek professional assistance and learn more about your condition. You will also want to make some lifestyle changes with your new circumstances. It will help you soon begin to feel changes and once more be in control of your condition instead of it controlling you.

Do Strong Feelings Consume You?

Strong emotions such as sadness, anger, or resentment can indeed take a toll on your mental and emotional well-being. When these feelings dominate your thoughts and actions, they can create a barrier to pursuing what is truly important in your life. You may find yourself caught in a cycle of negativity that drains your time and energy, leaving little room for personal growth or fulfillment. Recognizing this pattern is the first step toward reclaiming control over your emotional landscape.

What Can You Do About It?

If you identify with these overwhelming emotions, it's crucial to explore strategies that can help you regain balance. One powerful approach is to lean into your faith if you are a person of faith. Many find solace in the belief that they can relinquish their burdens to a higher power, allowing them to focus on healing rather than dwelling on pain. This act of surrender can be liberating and provide a sense of peace amidst turmoil.

In addition to spiritual practices, writing down your feelings can serve as an effective outlet for processing emotions. Journaling allows you to articulate what you're experiencing, which can lead to greater self-awareness and understanding. It also provides a safe space for reflection where you can confront difficult feelings without judgment.

The Importance of Connection

Moreover, do not underestimate the value of community and support systems. Accepting help from friends or family members can significantly lighten the emotional load you carry. Sharing your struggles with someone who cares about you fosters connection and reminds you that you are not alone in facing life's challenges. Many individuals have walked similar paths before you; their experiences can offer insights and encouragement as you navigate through your own difficulties.

Recommended Tips for Managing Negative Feelings

If negative feelings are controlling your life, consider implementing the following strategies:

- Write Down Your Feelings in a Journal: This practice helps clarify thoughts and emotions while providing an opportunity for catharsis.
- Express Your Feelings to a Close Relative or Friend: Sharing your experiences with someone trustworthy can alleviate feelings of isolation and promote healing.
- Challenge Your Feelings: Engage in self-reflection by questioning the validity of negative beliefs about yourself. Ask yourself questions like, "Is there really evidence to support such a negative view?" This cognitive restructuring helps shift perspectives.
- Redirect Your Energies: Instead of holding onto anxiety, anger, or resentment, channel those energies into productive activities—be it exercise, creative pursuits, or volunteering—which can foster positivity and purpose.

Bottom Line: Perspective Matters

Ultimately, it's essential to recognize that often, our negative feelings stem not solely from our circumstances but from how we perceive them. By shifting our perspective and employing practical strategies for emotional management, we empower ourselves to break free from the chains of negativity and pursue what truly matters in our lives.

Hope this was helpful.

You can change your current circumstances.

You Can Change Your Current Circumstances

If you were asked this question directly: How is life with you now? In other words, how do you view life now? How would you answer? This seemingly simple inquiry can evoke a myriad of responses, reflecting the diverse experiences and emotions individuals encounter in their daily lives. For some people, life is hard; they may be grappling with financial difficulties, health issues, or personal relationships that weigh heavily on their spirits. Others might describe their existence as bad, feeling trapped in a cycle of negativity or disappointment that seems insurmountable. Still, for others, life can feel boring—an endless routine devoid of excitement or fulfillment. If this resonates with your current feelings, I want to tell you today that life is good and could be better.

Only leopards cannot change their spots; thankfully, as human beings endowed with the capacity for growth and transformation, we are not bound by such limitations. Unlike the leopard's fixed nature, we possess the remarkable ability to redefine our circumstances and reshape our realities through conscious effort and intention. As a person who is focused and determined, you have the power to alter your perception of life by setting meaningful goals for yourself and striving towards the results you desire.

To embark on this transformative journey, it is essential first to engage in self-reflection. Take a moment to honestly assess your current situation. What aspects of your life bring you joy? What elements contribute to your dissatisfaction? By identifying these factors clearly, you can begin to understand what changes need to be made. Next, establish specific and achievable goals that align with your vision for a better life. These goals should be both short-term and long-term; they will serve as stepping stones toward creating the reality you wish to experience.

Moreover, it's crucial to cultivate a positive mindset throughout this process. Embrace challenges as opportunities for growth rather than obstacles that hinder progress. Surround yourself with supportive individuals who inspire and motivate you; their encouragement can significantly impact your journey toward change. Additionally, consider adopting new habits or skills that align with your aspirations—whether it's pursuing education in a field you're passionate about or engaging in activities that foster creativity and joy.

CHAPTER 6
THE ENERGY OF DETERMINATION

An example of perseverance in action is the invention of the electric light bulb. Thomas Edison faced the monumental task of inventing a practical and long-lasting electric light bulb at a time when there were no effective, reliable light sources that could be widely used. The technology was still in its infancy. Edison and his team conducted thousands of experiments to find the right materials for the filament and the best design for the bulb. It is reported that Edison failed over 1000 times before finding the right combination. Each time Edison encountered failure, he didn't view it as a failure but felt that he had just found 10,000 ways that wouldn't work. Edison would analyze what went wrong, learn from it, and adjust his approach accordingly.

The process took years of consistent effort, experimentation, and refinement. Despite numerous failures and skepticism from others, Edison remained focused on his goal. Edison's perseverance eventually paid off when he successfully invented a working light bulb with a carbonized bamboo filament that could last for 1200 hours. This invention not only changed his life but also revolutionized the world. Edison's story demonstrates that perseverance involves not just hard work but also resilience, learning from failures, and unwavering commitment to the end goal. Despite facing repeated failures, his ability to persist eventually led to one of the most significant inventions in history.

Every great achievement in history started with someone who didn't quit. Thomas Edison, JK Rowling, and even Michael Jordan. They all faced failures but kept going. Why? Because perseverance builds strength. It teaches you to adapt, to innovate, and to grow. When you persevere, you learn that failure is not the end; that's just a step toward success. Remember, every obstacle is an opportunity to improve. Each setback is a lesson in disguise. Break your ultimate goal into smaller manageable tasks. Each completed milestone will give you a sense of progress and motivate you to keep going. It also makes you understand and remind yourself regularly of the reasons behind your goal. This intrinsic motivation can sustain you during tough times. There, you will learn to accept and recover from setbacks. Viewing challenges as opportunities for growth can strengthen your perseverance and help you cultivate habits that align with your goal. We will now discuss seven steps to help build perseverance

1. Consistency, even in small actions, builds momentum over time.
2. Surround yourself with people who encourage and hold you accountable. Sharing your journey with others can provide motivation and valuable feedback
3. Focus on positive outcomes and visualize your success. This can keep you energized and focused on your goals.
4. Understand that reaching big goals takes time. Embrace the journey, and be patient with your progress.
5. Be open to learning from your experiences and adjusting your strategies. Flexibility in your approach can help you overcome obstacles.
6. Physical and mental health is crucial for sustained effort, regular exercise, and proper nutrition

7. Reward yourself for progress, no matter how small. Celebrating achievements can boost morale and reinforce your commitment. So don't be afraid to fail. Embrace the challenge and keep moving forward no matter what. In the end, your perseverance will lead you to your results beyond the goal because with perseverance, anything is possible

The Role of Belief Systems in Achievement

If we aim for success, it becomes essential to activate a belief system that aligns with achievement. This involves fostering an internal dialogue that encourages perseverance and resilience. For instance, when learning a new language or mastering a new skill, it is counterproductive to tell ourselves that it is too difficult or that we will inevitably fail. Such negative self-talk creates mental barriers before we even begin our journey, leading to a self-fulfilling prophecy where doubt breeds failure. Instead, adopt an empowering narrative that can transform challenges into opportunities for growth. By affirming our capabilities and visualizing success, we set the stage for positive outcomes. Research in psychology has shown that individuals who maintain a growth mindset—believing that their abilities can be developed through dedication and hard work—tend to achieve higher levels of success compared to those with a fixed mindset.

Therefore, cultivating a success-oriented mindset is vital for reaching our goals and crossing the finish line. This involves aligning our thoughts with those of successful individuals who have navigated similar paths. By studying their behaviors, strategies, and attitudes, we can emulate practices that lead to achievement while consciously refraining from adopting the habits of those who lack a success-driven mentality.

Moreover, planting seeds of positivity serves as both motivation and the driving force necessary for fostering a constructive mindset. Engaging in daily affirmations, surrounding ourselves with supportive individuals, and celebrating small victories are all effective strategies for reinforcing this positive outlook. When we focus on what we can control—our effort, attitude, and response to challenges—we empower ourselves. We will now discuss 10 Ways to Cultivate a Mindset of Success.

1. Embrace a Growth Mindset
Adopt the belief that your abilities and intelligence can be developed through dedication and hard work. This perspective fosters resilience and encourages you to view challenges as opportunities for growth.

2. Set Clear Goals

Define what success looks like for you personally rather than relying on societal expectations. Break down long-term goals into smaller, achievable milestones to maintain motivation and direction.

3. Reprogram Your Subconscious Blocks with Positive Self-Talk

Identify limiting beliefs that may hinder your progress and replace them with empowering affirmations. This shift in mindset can help unlock your full potential.

4. Build a Support Network

Surround yourself with positive influences, including mentors and peers who share similar goals. A supportive community can provide encouragement, inspiration, and constructive feedback.

5. Practice Meditation

Incorporate meditation into your daily routine to enhance mental clarity, focus, and productivity. This practice can also help reduce stress levels, contributing to a more successful mindset.

6. Cultivate Resilience with Kindness

Be kind to yourself when facing setbacks or failures. Practicing self-compassion allows you to bounce back more effectively and fosters a positive attitude towards challenges.

7. Celebrate Successes, Big and Small

Acknowledge your progress regularly by celebrating achievements along the way, no matter how small they may seem. Recognizing these wins boosts motivation and reinforces a success-oriented mindset.

8. Align with Your Values and Purpose

Ensure that your goals are in harmony with your personal values and mission in life. This alignment creates deeper motivation and connection to your work.

9. Avoid Comparison Traps
Focus on your unique journey instead of comparing yourself to others. Recognize that everyone has their own path, which helps maintain self-esteem and motivation.

10. Develop an Abundance Mentality
Shift from a scarcity-focused mindset to one that embraces limitless opportunities for growth and collaboration. Recognizing the abundance already present in your life fosters positivity and opens doors for success. Take actionable steps toward your goals

Finished what you start

The essential question is not merely when you initiated a task but rather whether you have successfully completed it. The significance lies in maintaining momentum and achieving a sense of fulfillment throughout the process. Are you someone who takes decisive action? If so, it's time to move forward and accomplish your goals. It's important to recognize that every beginning has an end; thus, reflecting on how you concluded your endeavors is crucial. Did you finish strong? Why does this matter?

Consider the example of attempting to escape from a detrimental situation or breaking free from a harmful habit. Are you still engaging in the same activities that once held you captive? It is vital to avoid falling back into those patterns, as doing so can lead to discomfort and stagnation.

In life, there are generally two categories of individuals: those who consistently make excuses and those who predominantly deliver results. Our internal dialogue often leads us to either feel guilty for not accomplishing enough or complacent because we believe we have done sufficient work. So, how can we prevent ourselves from feeling inadequate or making excuses? Here are three strategies to consider:

1. Run to the Finish Line: Commit yourself fully to completing your tasks with determination.

2. Run Past the Finish Line: Go beyond mere completion; strive for excellence and push your limits.
3. Run Indefinitely at the Finish Line: Maintain a continuous pursuit of improvement and growth even after achieving your initial goals.

By adopting these approaches, you can ensure that you not only start strong but also finish with purpose and clarity.

Keeping Pace With Time

You have likely heard the saying that time waits for no one. Regardless of our actions or intentions, time continues its relentless march forward. It is the very essence of life itself. This constant progression presents a challenge for individuals, as it establishes boundaries and limitations in our lives. The finite number of days we experience, the anticipation that fills the hours between day and night, and the cyclical nature of seasons all serve as reminders of time's authority over us.

Thus, it is essential to reflect on your own relationship with time: Are you ready to keep pace with its flow, move in a different direction, or remain stagnant? Are you adhering to the speed limits set by your circumstances, or do you choose to disengage and allow others—those who began their journey alongside you—to surpass you? This inquiry encapsulates the core message of this book: "My Results, Beyond the Finish Line."

You can approach this work as a valuable resource—a tool designed to empower you on your journey toward achievement. Let it serve as a companion, a partner, and a trusted friend throughout your endeavors. Whenever you find an opportunity, revisit the pages of "My Results Beyond the Finish Line" to draw inspiration and guidance

We often hear the phrase "time flies," and there is substantial evidence to support this notion, particularly when we are engaged in enjoyable activities or surrounded by friends. The fleeting nature of time can sometimes feel overwhelming; however, there is a silver lining—a beacon of hope. This hope lies in the understanding that we are the custodians of the time allotted to us. It is essential to recognize that we have the power to take control of our time and make conscious decisions about how we spend it.

While external circumstances may present challenges, it is crucial to remember that you alone determine your destiny when you seize control of your life. If you find yourself feeling stuck or stagnant, know that you possess the ability to alter your trajectory and change your course. Regaining control allows you to navigate toward your goals with clarity and purpose, keeping your aspirations firmly in mind.

Taking charge of your time means actively choosing the path that leads you to your desired destination. You hold the reins; only you can redirect your journey toward success. It is indeed possible for you to achieve your objectives if you commit to making proactive choices.

When contemplating your goals, it's essential to reflect on how you perceive them. If your aim is to achieve a state of comfort that lies beyond the finish line, it is crucial to take a moment to assess and evaluate all the activities that may be holding you back. By identifying these burdens and consciously deciding to leave them behind today, you can use this realization as motivation to propel yourself toward success.

Life is filled with uncertainties; many events occur that we do not fully comprehend, yet they shape our existence. Commitment plays a vital role in our journey. Just as we wouldn't leap from the summit of a mountain or a skyscraper only to discover the immutable force of gravity, we must recognize the fundamental truths that govern our lives. Nature operates within fixed parameters: rain falls, sunlight illuminates, trees grow, and oceans remain steadfast in their positions within the solar system.

However, one remarkable aspect of human life is its inherent flexibility; unlike natural phenomena, our lives are not predetermined or static. We possess the power to make adjustments, choices, and decisions that can significantly alter our paths. This ability empowers us to envision where we want to be and when we wish to arrive at those destinations.

In "Result Beyond the Finished Line," we are provided with a comprehensive set of tools designed to empower and prepare us for navigating our achievements beyond mere completion. This book encourages us to actively shape our own narratives of success, detailing the journey and motivations that propelled us past the finish line. As we engage with these concepts, we will start to perceive our surroundings through a more optimistic lens—envisioning clearer skies, improved conditions, and brighter days ahead. This shift in perspective ultimately leads to an enhanced quality of life, embodying the essence of results that extend beyond not just reaching our goal but also enjoying the benefits of the impact of reaching our results beyond the finished line.

The Importance of Standing for Something

In our lives, it is essential to take a stand for something meaningful; otherwise, we risk standing for nothing at all. Many individuals may never encounter the opportunity to assert their beliefs or values, but we find ourselves in a unique position where we can. The mere act of engaging with this book, My Result Beyond the Finished Line, signifies that we have the chance to take control of our future actions. This moment presents us with an opportunity to make choices that can propel us toward achieving our goals and ultimately crossing the finish line.

Recognizing the importance of standing firm in our convictions allows us to navigate life with purpose and intention. Each decision we make can lead us closer to realizing our aspirations. By actively participating in discussions, seeking knowledge, and reflecting on our values, we empower ourselves to take decisive steps forward. This proactive approach not only enhances our personal growth but also contributes positively to the communities around us.

As we move forward, let us embrace the potential that lies within each of us. By standing for something significant and seizing opportunities as they arise, we can shape our destinies and achieve fulfillment in both our personal and collective journeys.

A Call to Action

Now is the time to eliminate procrastination from your life—lock it away and discard the keys for good. To truly harness your potential, mastering time management and adapting to current circumstances is vital. By doing so, you can propel yourself beyond any point of no return. When you select a clear pursuit toward your finish line, success becomes attainable. Conversely, if you remain passive and fail to engage with the present moment, stagnation will be inevitable.

It is often more advantageous to experience a crash landing at the finish line and then take the time to recover and rebuild from the fragments of that experience rather than to meander aimlessly and become lost in inaction due to a refusal to engage. It is essential to recognize that certain opportunities are tailored for specific successes. Therefore, it is crucial to maintain momentum and keep moving forward. The adage about not crying over spilled milk remains relevant; dwelling on wasted time equates to years irretrievably lost. Consequently, it is vital to lock away past regrets and seize control of the present moment, allowing yourself the chance to compensate for any time that may have been squandered. Taking control involves understanding your available options and seeking assistance when necessary—this is where help becomes invaluable. We must avoid becoming mere spectators in our own lives or remaining passive observers on the sidelines. Instead, we will make a conscious affirmation today to actively engage in our lives. We will challenge ourselves to push beyond our limits, striving to do everything within our human capacity to ensure a brighter tomorrow, starting from this very moment.

CHAPTER 7
THE POWER OF PERSEVERANCE

In this chapter, we learn about the importance of perseverance through the story of Thomas Edison and his work on the electric light bulb. At that time, there were no good sources of light that people could use easily, and the technology for electric lighting was still very new. Edison faced a huge challenge in creating a light bulb that would last a long time and work well.

Edison and his team tried thousands of different experiments to find the right materials for the filament (the part inside the bulb that produces light) and to design the bulb itself. It is said that he failed over 1,000 times before he finally discovered what worked. Instead of seeing these failures as setbacks, Edison had a positive attitude; he believed he hadn't failed but rather found many ways that didn't work. Each time something went wrong, he would think about what happened, learn from it, and change his method for the next time.

This whole process took years of hard work, testing, and improving his designs. Even though he faced many failures and people doubted him, Edison kept his eyes on his goal and continued to push forward. Edison's determination eventually led him to create a functional light bulb that used a carbonized bamboo filament, which could last for 1200 hours. This invention not only changed his life but also transformed the world. Edison's journey shows that perseverance is more than just hard work; it includes resilience, learning from mistakes, and staying committed to your goals. Even though he faced many failures, his ability to keep going resulted in one of the most important inventions ever.

Every major success in history began with someone who refused to give up. People like Thomas Edison, JK Rowling, and Michael Jordan all encountered failures but continued to push forward. Why do they do this? Because perseverance builds strength. It helps you adapt, innovate, and grow. When you persevere, you realize that failure isn't the end; it's just part of the journey toward success. Keep in mind that every challenge is a chance to improve, and each setback offers a lesson in disguise. Breaking your big goal into smaller tasks makes it easier to manage. Each time you finish one of these smaller tasks, you'll feel like you're making progress, which can motivate you to keep going. It's important to remind yourself why you set this goal in the first place. This inner motivation can help you push through tough times. When you face setbacks, try to see them as chances to learn and grow, which can help you stay strong and develop habits that support your goal.

Seven steps to build perseverance

1. Be Consistent: Even small actions taken regularly can build up over time and create momentum.
2. Find Supportive People: Surround yourself with friends or mentors who encourage you and hold you accountable. Sharing your experiences with others can give you motivation and helpful feedback.
3. Visualize Success: Focus on positive results and imagine yourself succeeding. This mindset can keep your energy high and help you stay focused on your goals.
4. Be Patient: Understand that achieving big goals takes time. Embrace the process and be patient with how quickly or slowly you're progressing.

5. **Be open to learning from your experiences and adjusting your strategies. Flexibility in your approach can help you overcome obstacles.**
   Stay willing to learn from what happens to you and be ready to change how you do things. Being flexible can help you get past challenges.

6. **Physical and mental health are crucial for sustained effort; regular exercise and proper nutrition are essential.**
   Taking care of both your body and mind is very important if you want to keep working hard over time. Make sure to exercise regularly and eat well.

7. **Reward yourself for progress, no matter how small. Celebrating achievements can boost morale and reinforce your commitment. So don't be afraid to fail; embrace the challenge, and keep moving forward no matter what; in the end, your perseverance will lead you to your results beyond the finished because with perseverance anything is possible.**
   Give yourself a treat for any progress you make, even if it's tiny. Celebrating what you've done can lift your spirits and strengthen your dedication. Don't fear failure; accept the challenges, keep pushing ahead, and remember that sticking with it will eventually bring you success because if you don't give up, anything can happen.

Cultivating a Positive Mindset Toward Your Best Results

Having a positive attitude isn't just about hoping for good things; it's about making a space where success can happen. By getting rid of doubts about ourselves and believing in our abilities, we create opportunities for growth and success. As we work towards our goals, let's keep in mind that every thought we have plays a part in this journey. Every thought we have plays a role in shaping our life story, which is full of possibilities waiting to be discovered, meaning our growth mindset.

What is a Growth Mindset?

A growth mindset means believing that we can improve our skills and intelligence through hard work and dedication. This is different from a fixed mindset, where people think their abilities are set in stone and cannot change.

Having a growth mindset helps us become more resilient, motivated, and eager to learn. It encourages us to focus on effort rather than just natural talent, take risks, learn from our mistakes, receive helpful feedback, and build supportive environments where we can work together with others. To reach our goals, it's important to develop a mindset that helps us pursue our ambitions instead of holding us back. This involves understanding the differences between mindsets and promoting behaviors that lead to personal growth.

This means we should try not to doubt ourselves or question our skills as we move forward. Every word we say or think about our future can either help us grow or hold us back. How well we do in life is greatly affected by how we think, which can make a big difference in whether we succeed or fail.

If we want to be successful, it's important to have a belief system that supports achieving our goals. This means having positive thoughts that encourage us to keep going and stay strong. For example, when we're trying to learn something new, like a language or a skill, it doesn't help to tell ourselves that it's too hard or that we'll definitely fail.

Negative Self-Talk and Its Effects

Talking negatively to ourselves can create mental blocks even before we start working towards our goals. This often leads to a situation where our doubts cause us to fail, which then reinforces those doubts. Instead of this negative mindset, we should focus on positive thoughts that help us see challenges as chances to grow. By believing in ourselves and imagining our success, we prepare for better results.

Studies in psychology indicate that people who believe they can improve their skills through hard work—known as having a growth mindset—tend to be more successful than those who think their abilities are fixed and cannot change.

To achieve our goals and succeed, it is crucial to develop a mindset focused on success. This means thinking like successful people who have faced similar challenges. By observing how they act, what strategies they use, and their attitudes, we can adopt habits that lead to success while avoiding the behaviors of those who do not succeed.

Planting positive thoughts helps us stay motivated and build a good mindset. Doing daily affirmations, being around supportive people, and celebrating small wins are great ways to keep this positive attitude strong. When we concentrate on what we can control—like our effort, attitude, and how we deal with problems—we give ourselves more power. Now, let's look at ten ways to develop a successful mindset.

1. **Embrace a Growth Mindset**
   Believe that you can improve your skills and intelligence through hard work and dedication. This way of thinking helps you bounce back from setbacks and see challenges as chances to grow.

2. **Set Clear Goals**
   Decide what success means for you instead of following what society expects. Break big goals into smaller, manageable steps to help you stay motivated and focused.

3. **Change Your Negative Thoughts with Positive Self-Talk**
   Look for beliefs that hold you back and replace them with positive statements about yourself. Changing how you think can help you reach your full potential.

4. **Create a Support System**
   Surround yourself with positive people, like mentors and friends, who have similar goals. Having a supportive group can give you motivation, inspiration, and helpful feedback.

5. **Make Meditation a Habit**
   Add meditation to your daily life to improve your focus, clarity of thought, and productivity. It can also lower stress, which helps create a more successful mindset.

6. **Build Resilience Through Self-Kindness**
   Be gentle with yourself when things don't go as planned or when you fail. Being kind to yourself helps you recover better and keeps a positive outlook on challenges.

7. **Celebrate All Achievements, Big or Small**
   Regularly recognize your progress by celebrating every achievement along the way, no matter

8. **Align with Your Values and Purpose**
   Make sure your goals match what you truly believe in and what you want to achieve in life. When your goals align with your values, you will feel more motivated and connected to your work.

9. **Avoid Comparison Traps**
   Instead of looking at what others are doing, concentrate on your own path. Understand that everyone has their own journey, which helps you keep a positive self-image and stay motivated.

10. **Develop an Abundance Mentality**
    Change your thinking from focusing on what you lack to seeing the many opportunities available for growth and teamwork. Acknowledging the good things already in your life can boost positivity and help you take steps toward achieving your goals.

Did You Complete What You Started?

The key question is not just when you begin a task but whether you finished it successfully. It's important to keep moving forward and feel satisfied during the process. Are you someone who takes clear actions:

Here are three strategies to considered
1. **Run to the finished Line:** Make a strong commitment to complete your tasks with determination.
2. **Go Beyond Just Finishing:** Don't just complete your tasks; aim to do them really well and challenge yourself to improve.
3. **Keep Improving After Success:** Even after reaching your goals, continue to seek ways to grow and get better.

By using these strategies, you can ensure that you not only begin your tasks with energy but also finish them with clear purpose and direction.

Keeping Pace with Time

You've probably heard that time doesn't wait for anyone. No matter what we do or plan, time keeps moving forward. This ongoing flow is a fundamental part of life. It can be challenging because it sets limits on what we can achieve in our lives.

Time Flies

We often say "time flies," especially when we're having fun or with friends. This feeling is backed by evidence, as time seems to pass quickly during enjoyable moments. However, this can also make us feel overwhelmed at times. The good news is that we have control over our own time. It's important to realize that we can decide how we want to spend it.

Taking Control of Your Life

Even when life gets tough, remember that you are in charge of your own future if you take control of your life. If you're feeling stuck, understand that you have the power to change your situation and move in a new direction. By taking back control, you can work towards your goals with clear focus and purpose, keeping your dreams in sight.

Flexibility of Human Life

One amazing thing about being human is that we can adapt our lives; they are not set in stone like natural events. We have the ability to make choices and changes that can greatly affect our future. This means we can think about where we want to go and when we want to get there.

Tools for Success Beyond Completion

In "Result Beyond the Finished Line," we find a helpful collection of tools meant to prepare us for achieving more than just finishing tasks. The book encourages us to take charge of our own success stories, focusing on the journey and reasons that helped us succeed. As we explore these ideas, we'll start to see the world in a more positive way—imagining better situations and brighter days ahead.

Changing how we view things can greatly improve our lives. It's not just about reaching our goals; it's also about enjoying the positive effects that come from achieving those goals even after we've reached them.

The Importance of Standing for Something

In life, it's important to believe in something meaningful; if we don't, we might end up believing in nothing. Many people may never get the chance to express their beliefs or values, but we are in a special position where we can. By reading this book, *My Result Beyond the Finished Line*, we have an opportunity to take charge of what we do next. This is a moment for us to make decisions that can help us reach our goals and finish strong. Understanding why it's important to stand by our beliefs helps us live with purpose and direction.

It's important to stick to what we believe in because it helps us live with purpose. Every choice we make can bring us closer to our dreams. When we join conversations, learn new things, and think about what matters to us, we give ourselves the power to move forward confidently. This active way of living not only helps us grow as individuals but also makes a positive impact on the people around us.

As we continue on our paths, we should recognize the potential inside each of us. By standing up for important causes and taking advantage of opportunities when they come, we can influence our futures and find satisfaction in both our personal lives and in our communities.

A call to action

Now is the time to stop putting things off—make procrastination a thing of the past. To reach your full potential, it's important to manage your time well and adjust to what's happening around you. By doing this, you can push yourself beyond the limits you thought were unbreakable. When you choose a clear goal to work towards, achieving success becomes possible. On the other hand, if you stay inactive and don't focus on what's happening now, you will likely get stuck.

Sometimes, it's better to face challenges head-on and deal with the consequences later than to wander aimlessly and miss out on opportunities because you're not taking action. It's important to understand that some chances are meant for specific achievements. So, keep moving forward and maintain your progress.

The saying about not worrying over spilled milk still holds true; focusing on lost time means you're wasting even more years. Therefore, it's crucial to let go of past regrets and take charge of your current situation. This gives you a chance to make up for any time that has been wasted. Taking control means knowing what options you have and asking for help when you need it. Help is very important in this process. We should not just watch our lives pass by or stay on the sidelines as observers. Instead, we should decide today to actively participate in our lives. We need to push ourselves beyond our limits and do everything we can to create a better future, starting right now.

CHAPTER 8
UNDERSTANDING PRIORITIZATION

In life, figuring out what is most important to us is key to being successful and happy. It's important to realize that nothing can be the most important thing in your life unless you choose to make it so. This understanding gives you the power to take charge of your life and decide what really matters to you. Even if certain things like relationships, work, or hobbies take up a lot of your time now, it doesn't mean you have to stick with them forever. You always have the chance to grow and change if you're open to looking at what you prioritize and adjusting it.

To prioritize well, it's necessary to spend time thinking about what truly matters in your life. This means asking yourself important questions such as: What are my main values? What makes me happy? What do I want to achieve? To shape your future according to what you truly want, it's important to answer some questions honestly. By doing this, you can create a clear plan that reflects your real desires. Setting specific and measurable goals based on your thoughts is crucial because these goals act as clear signs guiding you toward success.

The Importance of Decision-Making

It's also vital to recognize that being indecisive can harm your progress. Studies show that people who can't make up their minds often don't achieve the best outcomes. To focus on what matters most, you need a strong mindset. This mindset doesn't just happen; it requires deliberate choices. When you decide which goals are more important than others, you establish a structure that helps you work more efficiently. This prioritization process involves making sacrifices; some goals may need to be delayed or even given up completely. It's crucial to understand that every commitment takes time and energy, which are limited resources.

Choosing Your Focus

When you decide what to pay attention to, you also choose what to pay less attention to in your life. This doesn't mean you ignore other important areas completely; it just means that some things will have to wait while you work on your main goals.

Clarity and Priorities

Having a clear idea of what's most important helps reduce feelings of being overwhelmed or confused. In a world full of distractions and many things demanding your time, knowing your priorities makes it easier to handle challenges. It also gives you the strength to say "no" when needed, allowing you to save your time and energy for activities that support your goals.

Remember that figuring out your priorities is not a one-time task; it's something you need to keep doing. Life changes all the time—new chances come up, and some things become less important. By regularly checking and updating your priorities, you can make sure they still match what you want as your life evolves.

It's essential to focus on what you want to achieve in life. By figuring out what is most important to you and dedicating your efforts to those goals, you can create a more meaningful and satisfying life. Take charge of this process; give yourself permission to chase after what truly matters to you, even if it means putting some other interests on hold for the time being. By prioritizing your goals, you set yourself up for success and happiness.

Be Firm in Decision Making

In life, everyone faces many choices that influence their journey and future. It's important to realize that making a choice is not the same as making a decision. A choice usually means picking from different options without much thought, while a decision involves actively choosing to follow a specific path. When people make decisions, they accept responsibility for what happens next. This means they recognize that each decision moves them from where they are now (point A) to where they want to be (point B).

Staying at point A should not be seen as the end unless it truly matches what someone wants in life. Life is always changing, and personal growth requires us to keep moving forward and evolving.

If you find yourself in a place that doesn't help you grow or achieve your goals, it's important to see this as a chance to make a change instead of feeling stuck. Moving forward means you need to learn new things, push your limits, and try different experiences.

To explain this better, think about a straight line connecting two points, A and B. While the quickest way between these two points is indeed a straight line, getting there requires focus and intention. You need to create clear plans and stay committed to them. This approach helps you overcome challenges more easily and reach your goals faster.

Setting clear goals is crucial for making good decisions. These goals act like markers on your journey from point A to point B, giving you direction and motivation. When you clearly outline your plans, you're essentially creating a roadmap that helps guide your actions and choices.

Taking Responsibility and Accountability

Taking responsibility means being accountable for the outcomes of your choices. It's important to understand that while outside factors can affect results, you are ultimately in charge of your actions. When you accept this accountability, it helps you bounce back from challenges. Instead of blaming others when things go wrong, people who take responsibility tend to look at what happened, learn from it, and change their approach.

Additionally, being accountable promotes honesty and integrity. It emphasizes that you should fully own your decisions, regardless of whether they lead to good or bad results. This sense of ownership helps you become more self-aware and encourages personal growth by motivating you to learn from what you've experienced.

In summary, taking responsibility isn't just about recognizing the choices you've made; it's also about being actively involved in making decisions with clear intentions and goals.

Moving from one stage in life to another (from point A to point B) involves ongoing learning, taking action, and challenging oneself. It means not just accepting a mediocre life when there are better opportunities for happiness and fulfillment available.

By establishing clear goals and concentrating on them while also being responsible for the results of their actions, people can handle life's challenges more successfully. Wanting a comfortable and satisfying life goes beyond just making a choice; it becomes a deliberate decision that involves taking responsibility. This mindset is a strong driver for personal development.

Understanding Your SWOT Analysis

When working towards your personal and professional goals, one helpful tool is the S.W.O.T analysis. This stands for Strengths, Weaknesses, Opportunities, and Threats. Each part of this analysis is important for making decisions and planning effectively. By looking closely at these four areas, you can understand yourself better and make smarter choices that help you reach your goals.

Strengths refer to what you do well or what advantages you have. Strengths are the positive qualities or resources you have that help you achieve your goals better than others. These can be things like skills, knowledge, experience, or personal characteristics such as being resilient or creative. Understanding your strengths is important because it allows you to use them effectively in different situations. For example, if you're good at communicating, you might do well in jobs that involve negotiation or teamwork. When you know what you're good at, it not only makes you feel more confident but also helps you find the best way to position yourself in competitive settings. This means you can take advantage of your abilities to stand out and succeed.

Weaknesses are the areas where you might struggle or lack resources. Weaknesses are internal issues that can slow you down in reaching your goals. These might be skills you haven't developed yet or resources you don't have that are important for success. To find out what your weaknesses are, you need to be honest with yourself and reflect on your abilities without being too hard on yourself. For instance, if managing your time is difficult, recognizing this as a weakness allows you to look for ways to improve, like using planning tools or techniques to work more efficiently. Knowing your weaknesses is crucial because it helps you focus on areas that need improvement and reduces the chances of facing obstacles… The third part of the S.W.O.T analysis looks at **opportunities,** which are outside factors that can help a business grow and succeed. **Opportunities** are chances for growth or improvement that you can take advantage of. These opportunities can come from various sources like trends in the market, new technologies, changes in laws, or shifts in what consumers want. By paying attention to these external factors, businesses can discover new paths to success. For example, if more people want eco-friendly products in your industry, this is a chance to create new offerings that meet those needs. By actively looking for these opportunities and being open to change, individuals and businesses can improve their chances of doing well in their fields. Finally, **Threats** are external challenges or obstacles that could hinder your progress. These challenges can come from various sources, such as competition from other people or companies, economic downturns, changes in laws and regulations, or any other factors that could risk your success. To identify these threats, it's important to carefully evaluate the external environment and understand how these challenges might affect your plans. For instance, if a competitor launches an innovative product that changes the market significantly, it becomes crucial to develop strategies to address this threat—this could involve creating new products or enhancing customer interactions. By examining all these aspects, you can create a clearer picture of your situation and develop strategies to succeed.

The Importance of Continuous Learning

Historical figures like King Solomon remind us that learning never really stops. In our busy lives today, where information is everywhere—from research studies to technical skills—it's crucial to keep learning so we can make smart choices based on our S.W.O.T analysis (Strengths, Weaknesses, Opportunities, Threats).

By exploring different types of information—like academic articles, industry reports, mentorship programs, or online classes—you can improve your understanding of yourself and the world around you. This knowledge helps you spot opportunities and prepares you to handle any challenges that may come your way.

Take Action

To effectively take action, it's important to understand your S.W.O.T analysis, which looks at your strengths, weaknesses, opportunities, and threats. This understanding helps you create practical strategies for moving forward. Instead of just reacting to problems or chances as they come up, having this analysis allows you to be proactive.

Once you've carefully evaluated what you're good at and where you need improvement, along with the opportunities and challenges in your situation, it's time to make decisions and take action. This might mean setting clear goals that play to your strengths while also working on improving your weaknesses through focused efforts.

Additionally, when it comes to taking advantage of opportunities, being flexible is key. You should be ready to change your plans as new information or situations arise. This adaptability will help you keep making progress toward your goals.

Mastering S.W.O.T analysis helps people understand where they currently stand and shows them ways to achieve future success. This is done by making informed choices based on a clear understanding of themselves and their surroundings.

Disconnect from Negative Influence

In life, the people we choose to be around can greatly affect our happiness and success. Just like electricity needs a good conductor to work well, our lives benefit from being surrounded by positive influences. If we spend time with people who bring us down or spread negativity, we might struggle to reach our full potential. This comparison highlights how important it is to have good relationships because they directly impact what we achieve.

Think about your friends: Who are they, and what do you talk about? Are your conversations positive and helpful, or do they tend to be negative and critical? The things we let into our lives—through friendships, discussions, or activities—are very important in determining our outcomes. It's crucial to pay attention to these influences since they can either help us move closer to our goals or hold us back.

Understanding a Farmer's Work and his own success
To better understand this idea, let's look at how a farmer grows rice. A good harvest doesn't just happen; it takes a lot of careful planning and hard work. The farmer needs to find the right piece of land, buy seeds and fertilizers, and spend time on important tasks like planting, watering, and taking care of the crops. Every single step is crucial for getting a good amount of rice.

In the same way, if we want to achieve success in our lives—whether it's improving ourselves, advancing in our careers, or feeling better emotionally—we need to actively do things that help us reach those goals. Just like a farmer can't expect a great harvest without putting in effort and caring for his plants, we also have to take charge of what affects our lives. This means we should make a conscious effort to cut out negative influences that could hold us back.

Creating a Positive Environment for Growth
To achieve our goals, it's important to surround ourselves with positive people who motivate us to improve and succeed. Engaging in deep conversations that challenge our thinking and emotions, along with participating in activities that match our dreams, helps us build a supportive environment.

The Importance of Choosing Our Influences
In summary, stepping away from negative influences isn't just about avoiding harmful relationships; it's about actively creating a space that encourages positivity and personal growth. By carefully choosing who we spend time with and what discussions we engage in, we can greatly improve our chances of success. Just like a farmer takes care of his crops to ensure they grow well, we must also take care of our minds and spirits by building positive relationships.

In any project or goal, whether it's something personal like a hobby or professional like a job, the idea of stakeholders is very important. Stakeholders are people or groups who care about what happens as a result of our efforts. This can include family members, parents, sponsors, mentors, close relatives, and friends—basically anyone who has a personal interest in whether we succeed or fail. Recognizing who our stakeholders are is vital because they often provide the support that can help us move forward or may even hold us back.

When thinking about our stakeholders, it's important to realize that their views might not always match ours. For example, if you have your own family, the choices you make can affect them directly. Parents might voice their worries based on their past experiences and concerns for your safety and happiness.

Sponsors often concentrate on how much money is involved and what kind of returns they can expect. Mentors, on the other hand, share advice based on their own experiences, both good and bad. Each person involved has their own unique perspective shaped by their life experiences and beliefs.

But what do we do when we talk to these stakeholders and realize they don't agree with our vision? This can be especially tough if we are very passionate about our goals. The strong emotions tied to pursuing something we care about can clash with the doubts expressed by those we love and respect. This situation brings up important questions: Should we give up on our dreams just to make others happy? Or should we continue pushing forward even when they doubt us?

Impact of Dissenting Opinions.

The truth is that hearing negative opinions from people who genuinely care can lead to feelings of discouragement and self-doubt. If our closest supporters are skeptical about what we're trying to achieve, it can create an inner struggle where we start questioning whether our ambitions are valid.

In challenging situations, it's important to handle our relationships carefully while keeping our goals clear. One good approach is to connect with positive people—those who motivate us and have a hopeful view of what we want to achieve. These could be supportive friends, colleagues who have successfully overcome similar obstacles, or mentors who encourage creativity and taking risks. Talking to these positive individuals can give us a new outlook that helps balance out any negativity we might face and builds our strength.

Additionally, being around encouraging people can strengthen our determination to reach our goals. Positive stakeholders usually provide helpful feedback that boosts our confidence instead of bringing it down. They remind us of the benefits that come from taking smart risks and aiming high with our ambitions.

It's important to recognize the worries of those who are skeptical about our plans, but we should also focus on building connections with people who encourage and support us. By finding a balance between listening to valid concerns and drawing inspiration from positive voices, we can create an environment that helps us grow and succeed.

In summary, managing relationships with stakeholders means carefully considering both the good and bad influences as we work towards our goals. By concentrating on those who motivate us while being open to helpful feedback from others, we set ourselves up for greater success in achieving what we want.

The Result Problem Tree

Understanding why you want to achieve certain results is important for your personal development and success. To tackle the challenges that prevent you from reaching your life goals, it's helpful to break these challenges down into three parts: the root cause, the main problem, and the effects. This organized method allows you to thoroughly analyze what is blocking you from getting what you want.

Identifying the Root Cause

The first step in this process is figuring out what you believe is the main reason you're not achieving your desired results. This could be due to various issues, such as lacking knowledge or skills, not having enough money, limited connections with others, not having a clear vision of what you want, or not having a solid plan. Each of these issues can greatly slow down your progress and create obstacles that feel very difficult to overcome. If you find yourself short on money, it can seem like a big problem. But if you see this as something that can be changed rather than just a fact of life, you can start looking for solutions. You could look into different ways to get funding, like applying for grants, starting a crowdfunding campaign, or finding investors who believe in your ideas. If you feel unprepared because you lack training or education, think about taking classes or finding a mentor who has successfully done what you're trying to achieve.

Identifying the Main Problem

After figuring out what's causing your difficulties, it's crucial to identify the main problem that comes from these causes. The main problem is usually a specific issue that stops you from making progress. For example, if your main issue is not knowing how to start a business, then your focus should be on learning the basics of business and creating a solid business plan.

This stage is about looking honestly at where you are in life compared to where you want to be. It involves asking yourself difficult questions about how committed you are and whether you're ready to put in the time and effort needed to overcome challenges.

Recognizing the Effects

The last part is about realizing the impact of both the main issues and their underlying causes. These impacts can show up as feelings of frustration, a lack of progress in personal growth, or even doubts about yourself. It's important to understand these effects because they can either push you to take action or make you feel stuck.

When faced with difficulties, it's easy to feel sorry for yourself. However, it's essential not to let those feelings control what you do. Instead of seeing challenges as barriers that stop you from moving forward, try to think of them as opportunities that can help you reach new heights. The main point is about how you react to difficulties. You can either let these problems stop you from moving forward, or you can use them as chances to improve and grow.

Taking Action: How to Overcome Challenges

When you face challenges, it's important to take action instead of just feeling sorry for yourself. Instead of letting difficulties like money issues or a lack of guidance hold you back, think about how these challenges can help you grow and change for the better. Here are some practical steps you can take:

Mindset Shift Changing your way of thinking is important. Instead of just trying to get by, focus on improving your situation.

Addressing Key Areas Take specific actions to tackle three main areas: the root cause of your problems, the main issue you're facing, and the effects those problems have on your life.

Position for Success: By doing this, you set yourself up not just to survive but to truly succeed and achieve your life goals.

Financial Limitations: Look for different ways to get funding or create a budget that works for you.

Lack of Space: Explore online options or shared workspaces that can help cut down on costs.

Insufficient Training: Dedicate time to online classes or workshops that can improve your skills.

No Mentor: Actively network with people who inspire you and are open to sharing their knowledge.

In summary, turning obstacles into opportunities requires determination and creative thinking in solving problems.

A Life Project Approach

When we look at our lives like a project, it becomes clear that keeping track of our progress is key to reaching our goals. Just like in any work project where we set goals and check off milestones, thinking of life this way helps us evaluate how we're doing in achieving our personal aims. This mindset promotes a methodical way to improve ourselves and accomplish what we want.

The Importance of Monitoring Progress

Keeping an eye on our progress is important because it shows us if what we're doing is actually helping us reach our goals. In project management, "inputs" are the resources—like time, effort, and money—that we use to achieve certain results. In our personal lives, these inputs can be things like education, relationships, health habits, and career efforts.

Investing Time Wisely

Sometimes, people spend a lot of time on a job that doesn't help them grow in their career or make them happy. On the other hand, you can be busy with activities that seem productive but don't give good results if you're not putting in enough effort. For example, if you exercise regularly but don't eat well, you might not see improvements in your health even though you are working out consistently. This shows that it's important to look at both how good the activities are and whether you're putting in enough resources like time and effort.

Tracking Progress Towards Goals

To keep track of your progress toward your life goals, it helps to have a clear plan. This means setting specific goals and figuring out how to measure your success along the way. Using tools like journals or apps can make this easier because they allow you to write down what you achieve and any challenges you face regularly.

Setting Key Performance Indicators (KPIs)

To better track your progress toward your goals, it's helpful to set specific measures known as key performance indicators (KPIs). For example, if your goal is to get fitter, you might look at things like how much weight you've lost or how fast you can run a certain distance. By regularly checking these measures over time, you can see patterns that help you know what changes you need to make.

Making Changes Based on Feedback

Checking in on your progress often allows you to make smart choices about what to do next. If some activities aren't giving you the results you hoped for or if you're not putting in enough effort, you can change things up. This could mean spending less time on activities that aren't helping and focusing more on those that are leading you toward your goals. You might also look for extra help, like finding a mentor or taking a class.

Additionally, it's important to have feedback loops—this means thinking about what's working well and what isn't. This reflection is crucial for ongoing improvement.

Talking to trusted friends or mentors can help you think more clearly about your life. They can offer different viewpoints that might help you reflect better on your experiences.

Treating Life as a Project

To make progress in life, it's important to see it as an ongoing project. This means you need to be dedicated to keeping track of how you're doing and making changes when necessary. By adopting this approach and using good ways to monitor your progress, you can navigate your life journey more effectively and improve your chances of reaching meaningful goals.

Planning and Evaluation in Personal Growth

Just like any successful project requires careful planning and checking how well things are going, our personal growth also needs attention to detail. We should regularly assess how we are progressing toward our life goals.

CHAPTER 9
OVERCOMING CHALLENGES

Facing Fear and Doubt

Fear and doubt are like invisible walls that can block you from reaching your goals. They manifest as negative thoughts in your head, telling you things like "You can't do this" or "What if you fail?" These feelings can be so overwhelming that they stop you from moving forward toward what you want to achieve. To truly overcome challenges, it's crucial to confront these fears and doubts directly.

Understanding Fear and Doubt

Fear is a normal reaction when faced with the unknown; it serves as a protective mechanism for your mind against possible dangers, whether they are real or imagined. In terms of personal growth and success, fear usually doesn't come from actual threats but rather from the fear of failing or being rejected. Doubt refers to the uncertainty you feel about your skills or the results of your actions. Together, fear and doubt form a mental barrier that can prevent you from even attempting to pursue your goals.

Face Fear and Doubt Heads On

Recognize Your Fears: The first thing you need to do when dealing with fear is to admit that you have it. It's normal to feel afraid, and acknowledging your fears is the first step toward overcoming them.

Question Negative Thoughts: Doubt often shows up as negative thoughts about yourself. You can fight these thoughts by asking if they are really true. Consider questions like, "Is this really accurate?" or "What's the worst that could happen?" You might discover that your fears are blown out of proportion and not as scary as they seem.

Take Small Actions: You don't always need to make huge changes to conquer your fears. Sometimes, just taking small steps toward what you want can help. Each little success can boost your confidence and lessen your fear.

Imagine Success: Visualization can be a strong technique. By imagining yourself successfully facing a challenge, you can lessen the fear tied to it. Your brain often can't tell the difference between real experiences and those you vividly imagine, so use this ability to help yourself.

Real-Life Examples of Overcoming Challenges

Think about Thomas Edison, who tried many times to invent the lightbulb but failed repeatedly. Instead of letting his fears and doubts stop him, he viewed each failure as a step toward success. His determination in the face of these setbacks eventually resulted in one of the most important inventions ever.

Another example is Oprah Winfrey, who dealt with many hardships in her life, such as growing up in poverty, experiencing abuse, and facing discrimination. Even with these challenges, she faced her fears and turned them into motivation. Today, she is a worldwide symbol of strength and shows how powerful it can be to overcome fear and doubt.

Learning From Failures

Failure is often seen as the opposite of success, but it is actually a crucial part of reaching your goals. Every successful person has faced failures at some point. What makes them different is their ability to learn from these experiences and use them to move forward.

Failure should not be viewed as the end; instead, it is an opportunity to learn. Each failure teaches us important lessons about what works and what doesn't. It encourages you to rethink your methods, make necessary changes, and try again with a better plan. Recognizing this can change how you view failure—from something scary to something valuable that can help you grow.

Strategies to Learn from Failure

1. **Reflect on the Experience:** After experiencing a failure, take some time to think about what happened. Consider what went wrong and what you could have done differently. Being honest with yourself during this reflection helps you learn valuable lessons from the situation.

2. **Identify the Lessons:** Every failure teaches us something. This could involve learning how to prepare better, make smarter decisions, or recognize your own limitations. Make sure to pinpoint these lessons and think about how you can use them in future situations.

3. **Adapt and Improve:** Use the insights you've gained from reflecting on your experience to change your approach moving forward. Remember that failure is not the end; it's just a chance to adjust your course as you work toward success.

4. **Maintain Resilience:** Resilience means being able to recover from difficulties. Build your resilience by keeping your long-term goals in mind and staying positive, even when faced with setbacks.

Real-Life Examples of Resilience

Think about Steve Jobs, who was kicked out of Apple, the company he helped start. Instead of letting this setback hold him back, he learned from it and grew stronger. He went on to create successful projects like Pixar before coming back to Apple, where he helped the company achieve amazing success.

Another example is J.K. Rowling, who faced many rejections before her Harry Potter books were finally published. Each time she was turned down, she learned something that helped her improve her story and keep trying until she succeeded. Now, her books are some of the best-selling ever.

Bouncing Back is Stronger

Resilience means being able to recover quickly from tough times and challenges. It's about having the mental strength to keep pushing forward even when things don't go as planned. Building resilience is important for overcoming obstacles because it helps you deal with difficulties without giving up. Resilience means being able to cope with difficulties rather than avoiding them. Life will always present challenges, whether they are personal issues, work-related problems, or unexpected events. Being resilient helps you face these challenges with strength and determination, allowing you to come out even stronger afterward.

Strategies to Build Resilience

Cultivate a Positive Mindset: People who are resilient tend to keep a positive attitude, even during hard times. Instead of focusing on the negatives of a situation, try to see the opportunities that come with it. Changing how you view setbacks can greatly influence how you deal with them.

Develop a Support System: It's important to have people around you who encourage and support you. A solid network of family, friends, or mentors can offer help and advice when you're going through tough times.

Practice Self-Care: Taking care of your physical and mental health is crucial for building resilience. Make sure to look after your body by eating healthy foods, exercising regularly, and getting enough sleep. Practicing mindfulness and using stress management techniques can also help you stay calm and focused during tough times.

Stay Flexible: Resilience means being able to adapt. Sometimes, to reach your goals, you need to change how you do things or take a different path. It's important to be willing to modify your plans when the situation calls for it.

Real-Life Examples

Nelson Mandela is a great example of resilience. He spent 27 years in prison fighting against apartheid but never wavered in his dedication to justice and equality. His ability to stay strong during tough times not only helped him endure but also enabled him to guide South Africa toward democracy and healing.

Another inspiring figure is Malala Yousafzai, who survived an assassination attempt by the Taliban because she stood up for girls' education. Instead of giving up out of fear, Malala continued her fight for education rights and became a worldwide symbol of strength and bravery. She won the Nobel Peace Prize and continues to motivate millions with her story.

Facing Challenges for Success

Dealing with difficulties is essential for achieving long-term success. When you confront your fears and doubts, learn from your mistakes, and develop strength to bounce back, you can handle life's hurdles more confidently. Each challenge you face can make you stronger, but what truly matters is how you react to those challenges.

The Importance of Clear Motives

Having clear reasons for what you want to achieve is a strong motivator that encourages action toward your goals. It's important to reflect on whether your motives are aligned with what you want to accomplish. Your motives often arise from wanting to solve a problem or meet a need in your life or the lives of others. To understand how motivated you are right now, think about how much energy and enthusiasm you have—would you say it's high, medium, or low? This self-assessment is crucial because your motivation can change based on different factors around you and within yourself.

When someone is unhappy with their life, this feeling can show up in how they look or act. For example, do you notice yourself frowning or looking down when things don't go your way? It's important to be aware of how you respond to these feelings of unhappiness because it can affect what you do next. Your reaction can either motivate you to chase your goals with enthusiasm or make you feel stuck and unmotivated.

The Role of Dissatisfaction in Change

How you handle challenges in life will influence your journey toward achieving what you want. If there are parts of your life that you're not happy with, this feeling can actually push you to make changes. It might spark a stronger desire in you to find answers and reach your true goals. However, it's also crucial to recognize that while we have a lot of potential for success, there are times when we face situations that we can't control—these are often referred to as "catch-22" situations.

Life can be unpredictable, and sometimes things happen that throw us off course. This means that when we set goals, we need to think about not just what we want to achieve but also the unexpected events that might come our way. It's important to pay attention to our environment and choose the right moments for our actions. By being aware and preparing ourselves, we can reduce the chances of finding ourselves in difficult situations. To reach our life goals, it's important to understand what drives us. This requires looking inward and recognizing how feelings of dissatisfaction can push us to strive for more. By being aware of our emotions and considering outside influences that could affect our journey, we can make better choices as we work towards success.

Building a Strong Mindset

As we navigate through life, having a stable and determined mindset is crucial. This helps us s Just like a strong ship can sail through rough seas, people need to stay committed to their goals in life. The idea of being "blown about by every wind" reminds us that outside distractions and difficulties can easily lead us off course. However, those who are determined and focused can overcome these challenges.

The Importance of Effort

A crucial part of being successful is realizing how important our involvement and effort are in what we do every day. Similar to a skilled worker who knows the benefits of finishing his job, each person should understand that the work they put in directly affects what they will achieve. This understanding creates a sense of responsibility and urgency, pushing us to take action instead of just watching life go by.

Staying on Track with Goals

To keep moving forward with our life projects, we need to regularly think about the results we want to achieve—these are our deliverables.

Purpose and Action

To achieve our goals, we need to stay focused on what we want to accomplish. It's important not to get distracted by temporary opportunities or other things that might come up. Instead, we should keep our attention on the specific outcomes we've planned for ourselves.

The Importance of Acting Now
Now is the time to take action; putting things off can hurt our chances of success. While it might seem like missing out on opportunities in the past doesn't matter much, it's crucial to understand that if we don't act on what we've learned today, we might regret it later.

Knowledge and Change
Reading motivational books or consuming inspiring content can help us change for the better. However, if we don't take action based on that knowledge, it won't make a difference in our lives.

Importance of Stability and Focus
When working towards our life goals, it's crucial to stay stable and focused. This means we should fully dedicate ourselves to what we're trying to achieve and take action right away based on what we've learned. The path to success can be tough, but if we remain determined and clear about our goals, we can overcome any difficulties that come our way. Embracing stability and focus is paramount when pursuing life goals. By committing ourselves fully to our endeavors and taking immediate action based on what we have learned, we position ourselves for success. The journey may be fraught with challenges, but with unwavering determination and clarity of purpose, we can overcome any obstacle that stands in our way.

CHAPTER 10
RESULTS BEYOND THE FINISHED LINE- EMBRACING NEW PATH?

In our journey through life to get the Results we truly desire and are working hard achieve, we may often encounter moments that may seem like dead ends—situations where growth or success feels out of reach. However, it's essential to recognize that these moments are not the end; they are simply opportunities for transformation. A "dead end" can be likened to a road that appears to have no exit, but it is crucial to understand that every obstacle presents a chance for redirection and innovation.

When faced with challenges, whether they manifest as obstacles in our careers or personal relationships, we must remember that there is always a way forward. Instead of feeling stuck, we can choose to change our course and explore new avenues. The world is full of possibilities waiting to be discovered. Our time, resources, and skills are not fixed; they can expand and evolve through strategic management.

By prioritizing what truly matters, delegating tasks effectively, automating processes where possible, seeking innovative funding strategies, investing in training to enhance our skills, and embracing the latest technologies, we can unlock new potentials within ourselves. The key lies in our mindset—viewing setbacks as steppingstones rather than barriers.

Let us embrace the journey with resilience and creativity. Remember, there are no dead ends for those who move beyond perceived limitations. Every challenge is an invitation to grow stronger and wiser. So, when you encounter what seems like a dead end, remember: it's merely a chance to forge a new path toward your goals.

To those who are truly focused on surpassing their goals understand that progress is not always in a straight line; sometimes the path forward requires redirection, recalibration, or a change in strategy. Note also that a dead end is only a mindset, a temporary pause in the journey, and not an ultimate barrier. The relentless pursuit of results beyond what seems like the finish line demands a belief in endless potential and the ability to turn every roadblock into a steppingstone for greater achievement. When the journey continues, so does the possibility for greater outcomes, ensuring that no road, no matter how challenging, is ever going to stop us from getting our results beyond the finished Line.

To truly embrace the pursuit of results that extend beyond ordinary expectations, it's essential to reject the finality of setbacks. Every obstacle is a chance to redefine the limits of personal and professional growth. Whether through creative problem-solving, shifting perspectives, or seeking new resources, those who persist understand that life's journey is dynamic and fluid. What may seem like an impassable barrier can, with the right mindset, become a pivotal turning point.

The key to avoiding dead ends lies in the refusal to accept limitations as absolute. Success often resides in perseverance, adaptability, and the courage to venture into uncharted territory when the conventional path seems blocked. This unwavering belief that there is always a way forward, even in the face of adversity, defines the difference between those who stop at the finish line and those who achieve results far beyond it.

A so-called dead end should prompt innovative thinking, fostering the resilience needed to explore alternate paths and discover opportunities that were once unseen. Therefore, however the road may twist and turn, but for the committed, there will always be a way to keep moving forward—because in their journey they understand, there is no such thing as a dead end.

THE CONCLUSION
EMBRACE YOUR JOURNEY BEYOND THE FINISH LINE

If you have reached this far, it is a testament to your resilience and determination. You have cultivated a mindset that is primed for success, one that propels you beyond the finish line. However, this is not the moment to rest on your laurels; instead, it is time to harness that momentum and push forward with even greater intensity. We must remain vigilant and proactive because life can change in an instant. Opportunities are fleeting, and we cannot afford to leave our future to chance. The days ahead may feel like they are closing in on us, but together, we can seize every moment and create our own opportunities.

Join me on the Result Train—there's plenty of room for everyone who is willing to strive for greatness! Stay focused on your goals and break them down into manageable mini-goals. Understand your SWOPT (Strengths, Weaknesses, Opportunities, Threats) so you can navigate challenges effectively. Remember that procrastination is a thief of time; it will undoubtedly slow your progress. Take action now: jot down your thoughts, document your journey through journaling, and adhere strictly to your plans.

Always keep in mind that while time may fly by, you are the pilot of your own life. You hold the reins and determine the direction you take. Time itself is fixed in its infinite nature; it will continue its course regardless of our actions. Therefore, make every moment count! Embrace this journey with passion and purpose—your future self will thank you for it!

Embrace the Power of Proactivity

In our fast-paced world, keeping pace with time is not just a necessity; it's a powerful strategy for success. To truly thrive, we must be proactive in our approach to life and work. One effective method is journaling, which allows us to set clear tasks with specific deadlines. By establishing a rigid timeline for our activities—perhaps aiming to complete a task within three days—we create a sense of urgency that propels us forward. This focused approach ensures that we utilize the remaining time wisely, allowing us to tackle other unfinished business without feeling overwhelmed.

When we leave our schedules open-ended, believing we have an entire week to complete tasks, we often fall into the trap of complacency. This can lead to procrastination, where we drift away from our goals and fail to achieve the results we desire. It's crucial to recognize that habits we've developed over the years can feel like unbreakable chains holding us back from making meaningful progress. However, here's the empowering truth: even the strongest chains can be broken!

While it may be challenging to change ingrained habits, there are tools and strategies available that can help us overcome these obstacles. Whether it's adopting new productivity techniques or seeking support from others, every step taken towards breaking free from these limiting patterns brings us closer to achieving our dreams. Remember, you have the power within you to transform your life and reach beyond the finish line—embrace it!

Breaking Habits and Embracing Change

Imagine a world where individuals have triumphed over their challenges—where people have successfully quit smoking, reduced alcohol consumption, achieved their fitness goals, learned to save money, completed projects, finished their schooling, and made wise investments. This is not just a dream; it is a reality that countless individuals have embraced. Yes, every bad habit you consider can be broken!

Right now, you possess the tools necessary to propel yourself beyond the finish line. The power to change lies within your grasp. What will you do with this opportunity? Keep the momentum going! Continue reading and absorbing knowledge because the next step is crucial: applying what you've learned. Trust in the process; it has the potential to shatter every chain that holds you back. You are capable of transforming your life, and this journey starts with a single decision to take action.

Every small step count towards your ultimate goal. Remember that persistence is key; even when faced with setbacks, each effort brings you closer to success. Embrace the challenges as they come and recognize that they are part of your growth. With determination and focus, you can break free from any limitations and create a life filled with achievements and fulfillment.

So, take a deep breath, believe in yourself, and move forward with confidence. The path may not always be easy, but every stride you take will lead you toward a brighter future where your dreams become reality.

Embrace a Positive Mindset

As we stand at the crossroads of our lives, it is essential to cultivate a positive outlook for the future. This mindset acts as a beacon, guiding us through challenges and illuminating pathways that may otherwise remain hidden. Without this optimistic perspective, we risk remaining shackled by our circumstances, unable to break free from the chains that bind us. Remember, every great achievement begins with a vision—a belief that something better lies ahead.

Take Action and Engage

The truth is simple: when we do nothing about our problems, nothing changes. Inaction breeds stagnation: however, when we choose to take action—no matter how small—we begin to engage with our lives actively. This engagement sparks momentum and creates opportunities for growth and transformation. It is in these moments of involvement that we discover our potential and realize that change is not only possible but within our grasp.

Learn from Experience

People often find themselves trapped in cycles of repetitive behavior. When you engage in the same actions without reflection, you can expect to receive the same results. If those results leave you feeling unfulfilled or dissatisfied, it's time to reassess your approach. Embrace the idea that change is necessary for progress; by altering your course and trying new strategies, you open yourself up to different outcomes—outcomes that can propel you beyond the finish line of your goals.

Prioritize and Invest in your self

Let's delve into some key concepts that can help guide this journey toward success—one of which is Pareto's Principle or the 80/20 rule. This principle teaches us to prioritize effectively by focusing on the 20% of efforts that yield 80% of results. By identifying what truly matters in your pursuits, you can allocate your time and energy more wisely, ensuring that each step forward brings you closer to your aspirations.

Investing in yourself is one of the most powerful decisions you can make. This investment comes in many forms: acquiring new skills, building assets, leveraging opportunities, expanding networks, and connecting with influential individuals who align with your vision. Each connection made adds value to your social capital and enhances your ability to navigate life's complexities.

Cultivate Ambition

Ultimately, let ambition be your driving force. Ambition fuels passion and determination; it pushes you out of your comfort zone and encourages continuous growth. As you strive for greatness, remember that every step taken towards self-improvement contributes not only to personal success but also inspires those around you.

Therefore, adopting a positive outlook for the future empowers us to break free from limitations and embrace change as an ally rather than an adversary. By taking action, learning from experiences, prioritizing effectively, investing in ourselves, and cultivating ambition, we set ourselves on a path toward achieving extraordinary things.

Investing in ourselves: A Path to Health and Wealth

To conclude, investing in ourselves now also means investing in our health. This is not just a necessity; it is a critical step toward achieving our best results and pushing beyond the finish line of our goals. Health and wealth can both be viewed as significant investments that yield long-term returns. When we prioritize our physical and mental well-being, we are essentially laying the foundation for a higher quality of life.

Imagine waking up each day filled with energy, ready to tackle challenges head-on. This vitality comes from making conscious choices about our nutrition, engaging in regular exercise, seeking mental health care when needed, and embracing preventive medicine. Each of these elements plays a pivotal role in enhancing our overall well-being. By nourishing our bodies with wholesome foods, we fuel our minds and spirits, enabling us to perform at our peak.

Moreover, regular physical activity not only strengthens our bodies but also boosts our mood and cognitive function. It's a powerful antidote to stress and anxiety, which can otherwise hinder our progress toward financial success or personal fulfillment. Mental health care is equally important; it equips us with the tools to navigate life's ups and downs effectively.

Preventive medicine ensures that we catch potential health issues before they become obstacles on our journey.

When you invest in your health, you increase your energy levels, extend your longevity, and enhance your overall productivity. These benefits create a ripple effect that positively influences your wealth accumulation and life satisfaction. The more vibrant and capable you feel, the more likely you are to pursue opportunities that lead to financial growth and personal achievements.

In essence, viewing health as an investment rather than an expense transforms how we approach self-care. It empowers us to take charge of our lives with intention and purpose. So let's commit today to prioritize our well-being—because every step we take towards better health is a step towards greater wealth and fulfillment.

Embrace Life and Purpose to the end.

Finally, let us take a moment to reflect on the profound importance of our existence. It cannot be emphasized enough that we aspire to live longer, not just to savor the fruits of our labor but also to thrive in good health. Our lives are precious, and each day presents an opportunity to fulfill our unique purpose, chase our dreams, and answer the callings that resonate within us. Imagine the countless brilliant ideas, aspirations, and ambitions that lie dormant in the graveyards—unrealized potential that could have changed lives or inspired generations. This stark reality serves as a powerful reminder: we must be alive and vibrant to bring our visions to fruition. The conclusion is clear: let us commit ourselves to living fully, passionately pursuing our goals, and ensuring that we cross the finish line with our results in hand. Together, we can transform dreams into reality and leave a lasting impact on the world.

BIBLIOGRAPHY

"The 7 habits of highly Effective People by steven R. Covey
This book emphasizes principles of personal effectiveness including proactive behavior and prioritization based on values rather than urgency.

Mindset: The New Psychology of Success " by Carol S. Dweck
Dweck's research highlights the importance of having a growth mindset versus a fixed mindset which directly influences how individuals approach challenges and setbacks.

The Lean Startup" by Eric Ries
Ries introduces concepts related to innovation management including validated learning through experimentation which aligns with acting based on feedback for continuous improvement.

Harvard Health Publishing
This source provides evidence-based information on health and wellness topics, emphasizing the importance of maintaining good health for a fulfilling life.

Psychology Today
A reputable publication that explores various aspects of human behavior and motivation, offering insights into how purpose and passion contribute to overall well-being.

The World Health Organization

An authoritative global health agency that focuses on public health issues and promotes healthy living as essential for achieving personal goals and societal contributions.

The WHO provides comprehensive information on global health standards and practices, emphasizing the importance of physical activity and nutrition for overall well-being. CDC The CDC offers valuable insights into preventive healthcare measures and mental health resources that support individuals in maintaining their health as an investment for future success. Harvard Health Publishing presents research-backed articles on the connections between physical fitness, mental wellness, and their impacts on productivity and life satisfaction.

American Psychological Association (APA)

The APA provides extensive research on behavior change and habit formation, offering insights into how individuals can effectively break bad habits through psychological strategies.

Mayo Clinic

Mayo Clinic provides comprehensive resources on health-related topics including fitness goals and financial wellness strategies, emphasizing practical steps for achieving personal objectives.

Mind Tools

MindTools is a comprehensive resource for personal development tools including SWOPT analysis and journaling techniques aimed at enhancing focus and productivity.

"Man's Search for Meaning" by Viktor E. Frankl

This book explores the importance of finding purpose in life, emphasizing how individuals can derive meaning even in challenging circumstances.

"Drive: The Surprising Truth About What Motivates Us" by Daniel H. Pink
Pink discusses intrinsic motivation and how autonomy, mastery, and purpose drive human behavior, providing insights into personal fulfillment.

"The Power of Habit" by Charles Duhigg
Duhigg examines the science behind habits and how understanding them can lead individuals to create positive changes in their lives and communities.

The Greater Good Science Center
An academic research center at UC Berkeley dedicated to studying the psychology of well-being including how acts of kindness contribute to personal happiness and social benefits.

Stanford Social Innovation Review
An authoritative source dedicated to exploring innovative solutions for social change through research articles focused on philanthropy and social impact initiatives.